So you want to go cy
A beginner's guide.
Peter Adcock

"Cyclers see considerably more of this beautiful world than any other class of citizens. A good bicycle, well applied, will cure most ills this flesh is heir to." — *Dr. K. K. Doty*

The rented Galaxy waiting for the ferry in Oban (2019).

Contents

Introduction

Sustrans Coast and Castle and NCN Route 1 signs.

If you're reading this I'm assuming you'd like to try cycle touring or you've tried it but want some hints and tips to make it more fun. If you're an experienced tourer, I'm flattered and thanks for reading this.

Maybe you're not sure where to go, what to take, which sort of bike you need, when to go, how to carry all that stuff or where to lay your head at night.

This is based on my experiences over the years, I'm not suggesting it's the correct way but it is a way. Hopefully this will begin to make it clearer for you; at least you should be on the right road so to speak. Consider this more of a set of thought starters in a "crikey I hadn't thought of that" kind of way with the final decision up to you. Feel free to disagree with absolutely everything I write of course if that helps!

If you need more information or clarification, I'm on social media (contact details provided in "About the Author") and I'm more than willing to exchange emails or have a phone call if that helps.

I use kit lists as a start point to deciding what to take but until I sat down and started typing, I didn't realise how much else I knew and did automatically. It doesn't matter whether I'm travelling solo or in a group, the things to consider are the same. I thought I'd share it with any folk considering a cycle tour.

🚲

Each chapter attempts to answer a question, most of the questions are open ended and I'm sure if you asked the same set of questions to 50 cyclists you'd get 50 different answers. A lot of it is a matter of opinion, what suits you and what type of trip you want to take.

If you need any more information on a particular topic, there is a wealth of knowledge out there; the internet is a great tool for looking at where others have gone and how they did it with blogs, websites and magazine articles to inspire you.

🚲 🚲 🚲

By way of background.

I've always cycled, to school, university (when it wasn't the trendy thing to do) and work as well as for pleasure. When at school in the 1970s we didn't go touring, it was a case of "anybody fancy cycling to Bournemouth for the weekend?". Having been brought up in Southampton we had plenty of options including hopping on a ferry to France for a couple of days with bike and tent. At the time we didn't realise we were "touring", it was just a bit of fun.

5

🚲

Since those school days, I've been on holiday on my bike off and on for over forty years and once or twice a year for the last twenty years. I guess you could say I'm an experienced cycle tourist but unlike some, I've never been away for weeks and months on end or anywhere outside Europe.

I've cycled solo, with a group for a couple of days up to a couple of weeks in the UK, France and Germany. An internet search will produce many names of hardy long distance tourers who go off for weeks and months including Mark Beamont, Andrew P Sykes, Tim Moore and Tom Allen, all of whom have completed some epic rides. I'm more of a "week or two" type of tourist, doing something fun and different but not away for long periods, however, Lands End to John O'Groats (LeJog) is very much one ride I would like to complete.

🚲 🚲 🚲

By anybody's standards, 2020 was a strange year with most of it spent battling an invisible virus (the early part of 2021 is continuing in the same vein). Restrictions followed by a spring lockdown resulted in many businesses closed or operating in new ways with the travel and hospitality

🚲

industries particularly badly hit. Travel was virtually nonexistent but cycling boomed with cycle sales higher than ever and cycle shops have never been so busy. Lockdown provided a great boost for cycling with empty or very quiet roads enticing people onto bikes. Something good may have come out of something bad, only time will tell.

After cancelling two proposed trips, one with my usual group and one solo, I was resigned to no touring in 2020. All of a sudden a window opened up in August and I did manage to cycle from Tynemouth to Edinburgh along the Sustrans Coast and Castles (south) route.

While thinking about potential trips in 2021, it occurred to me it doesn't matter who you are, where you're going and for how long, there are a set of common things which should be considered for a successful tour. It doesn't matter if you're touring for two days, two weeks or two months, you're still out there exploring on your bike. The same decisions have to be made in terms of where to go, for how long, where to stay, how to get there and back, what to take, how to carry it, what bike to use – so many questions!

How much planning you do is a personal choice of course but like many blokes of my age, I do love a list and have lists which are invaluable for planning the next adventure. I've also learned a few things over the years, some dos and don'ts as well as some things I could do if I ever decide to change my approach.

As I'm at home in Bristol during the 2021 lockdown, I thought I'd put my thoughts on paper in the vain hope they might be useful for anybody wanting to travel when we've finally got rid of this virus.

This is in no way an endorsement of any type of trip or gear; one brand over another but as in many things you get what you pay for when it comes to cycling gear. Having said that, Aldi and Lidl do have some excellent clothing bargains in their spring and autumn promotions.

My experience is limited in certain areas, for instance, I've camped a good deal while on the road but don't take cooking equipment. If this is your bag then I'll have to leave you to do your own research on what cooker etc to take.

This is aimed at the beginner or novice, someone who just needs that final push to saddle up and pedal off for a few days. There are plenty of accounts of long and short distance cycling, the concept is the same however but by definition, on a long distance trip, the cyclist is away for longer, must be more self sufficient and may have to deal with extremes of weather, terrain, local customs and border crossings.

In recent years, the choice of destination and anything bike-related including bikes themselves, bags, tents, equipment and navigational aids has become mind blowingly huge. A search for (say) "bike lights" will produce an eye watering number of options.

Let's try and make some sense of it all.

Why go cycle touring & what is cycle touring?

Canal du Midi 2010, with scenery like this, why not go cycle touring?

First of all, maybe it's good to have a think about what exactly cycle touring is. Cycle touring can be anything you want it to be, any distance, any destination, by any means provided you're on a bike and taking the trip for pleasure rather than sport. It attracts people from all walks of life, ages, both sexes, in groups or solo, hugely experienced or a first timer. You can ride a few miles or kilometres per day or hundreds; you can choose to sleep in a fancy hotel each night or camp cheaply or maybe even for free.

It's all about the cycling, you and your bike. The choice of destination, where to stop, where to sleep and when and what to eat is all up to you and your group. As long as you're waking up in a different place each day then you can consider yourself a cycle tourer.

Is Lands End to John O'Groats (LeJog) at 100 miles a day, while fully supported by a crew in a van really a tour? Maybe it is, but is it fun? Will you see and appreciate new places and have new experiences? Probably not, LeJog will be at least a 3-week trip for me!

While cycle touring typically involves overnight stays, a tour could be a long single-day bike ride; a multi-day event where your gear, food and clothing is carried in a vehicle which meets you at various checkpoints along your route; or a solo or group adventure where all clothing, equipment, food and tools are carried by you on your bicycle.

Maybe you see bicycle touring as a challenge, possibly to ride a certain number of miles or kilometres or maybe to reach a goal, to prove you can do it. Maybe it's a chance to get out into nature and experience the beauty of the countryside, or a way to lose weight and / or get into better physical shape.

Whatever your reasons, it's a unique means of seeing your surroundings, a fun and interesting way to meet other people and a chance to get away from your work and other responsibilities.

Bicycle touring can be all these things, it's true! But bicycle touring isn't always easy, especially if you're just starting out and don't have anyone to guide you through the process. You will make mistakes, forget to pack something, lose something, take a wrong turn or cycle into a bush as my mate did while trying to have a conversation with the person next to him. In my experience, things always work themselves out.

Cycling allows you to get off the beaten track and take routes unavailable to cars, motorbikes and public transport. You'll see far more of the countryside (and sometimes cities) from a different perspective, you can stop and admire a view (don't forget to stop for cake and coffee at every opportunity) whenever you wish and you're very likely to meet some interesting people.

🚲

There's certainly a sense of "two-wheeled road camaraderie", a special empathy amongst those who, like you, are experiencing a similar trip. I've met cyclists having problems and have stopped to offer my help (mostly it's politely declined), be it puncture repair, navigation problems or in one case, running repairs to somebody else's derailleur gears. On my Coast and Castles trip, I took a wrong turn and found myself on the A72, a main road, for a couple of miles when a motorcyclist drew alongside me to check I was OK. I was and in fact the A72 wasn't that bad.

People love to categorise all things cycling, put things in neat boxes; I'm not a fan. There are a few words bandied around but cycle touring is anything and everything you want it to be.

🚲 🚲 🚲

Cyclists have "toured" for as long as there have been bikes, with the Victorians embracing the new fangled velocipede. In Britain, the Cyclists Touring Club (rebranded Cycling UK in 2016 - see cyclinguk.org for more details) was founded in 1878 with 80 members growing to 70,000 by 2011. Cycling UK is now the biggest body campaigning for cycling and

🚲

cyclists' rights in the UK and continues to organise group touring events including day rides through its local groups. Both Cycling UK and British Cycling (britishcycling.org.uk) are useful resources.

The first proper cycle tourist could have been John Mayall who, in 1896, set out with two friends to cycle from London to Brighton, 30 miles into the journey, the friends gave up but John continued. This was the longest recorded cycle journey and maybe the first ever tour?

Jack Thurston, the author of "Lost Lanes: 36 Glorious Bike Rides In Southern England" wrote a good summary (A Thousand Freely Chosen Paths – A History of Cycle Touring) of the birth of cycle touring; see pannier.cc for more details. He attributes the introduction of the "safety bicycle" (with two equally sized wheels) in the 1880s which replaced the Penny Farthing as the start of the boom.

Although modern tourists have access to high tech mapping, GPS, various Apps, many well marked cycle paths and riding high tech bikes, bicycle touring has remained pretty much the same from its inception. A bicycle, a rider and a distant point on the horizon is all it takes to get started. Just mount your trusty steed and start pedaling.

🚲 🚲 🚲

There are many terms to describe types of touring which have become popular in recent years. Here's my attempt to decipher some. It's important to be clear on what type of tour you wish to undertake as the style of trip will influence what gear you need to take, how much gear, how you pack and of course which type of bike to use and how it should be configured. Don't get too bogged down in the words but think about what type (or hybrid) of tour is best suited to you.

Lightweight / credit-card / ultralight touring.

The cyclist carries the minimum of equipment and a credit card or cash while staying overnight in youth hostels, hotels, pensions, Gasthaus etc or B&Bs. Food is bought at cafes, restaurants or markets so only clothing etc needs to be taken.

Fully loaded / self-supported touring.

Cyclists carry everything needed, including food, cooking equipment and a tent (if camping). Some cyclists minimise

🚲

their load, carrying only basic supplies, food and a Bivouac shelter or lightweight tent. There is no outside support.

Expedition touring.

Cyclists travel extensively, often through developing nations or remote areas. The bicycle is loaded with food, spares, tools and camping equipment so the traveller is largely self-supporting.

Mixed Terrain Cycle-Touring / Bikepacking / Rough riding.

Cyclists travel over a variety of surfaces, often adopting an ultralight camping approach and carrying minimal gear (bikepacking). Cycle touring and bikepacking are often used interchangeably but it tends to be the type of bicycle, the type of road, the bicycle and how the gear is carried which sets them apart.

Supported touring.

Cyclists are supported by a motor vehicle which carries most of the equipment. This can be organised independently by groups of cyclists with a friend or family member driving the support vehicle, or commercial holiday companies selling places on guided tours. The guided trips usually include booked accommodation, luggage transfers, route planning and often meals and hire bikes maybe with mechanical support. Some companies provide accommodation and route information to cyclists travelling independently while others focus on a group experience, including guides and support for a large number of riders cycling together. A variation on this are holidays, often in exotic locations, organised in partnership with a charity, in which participants are expected to raise donations as well as cover their costs. This style of touring allows you to carry only what you need for a day of riding.

So, which type is for you?

What type of tour should I attempt?

Outer Hebrides, Luskentyre Beach, no words needed (2019).

A difficult question maybe but one that's easy to answer with a bit of thought. Ask yourself a few questions and the answer should fall out of the bottom. Having said that, it's fairly easy to plan a tour, pick a date, get a bike and maybe a tent and sleeping bag, choose a direction and start pedalling.

What type of tour takes your fancy?

The first thing to consider when deciding to start bike touring is what type you want to take , is it to be a quick weekend away or the fully supported tour around the vineyards of France?

Maybe as a first timer it might be wise to stay close to home; pick relatively easy terrain and climate (wait until after Easter!). If you're looking at a more ambitious project, find time to build up fitness and get in a few days practice beforehand. My first "tour" was as a teenager, setting off with a couple of friends towards the New Forest for a long weekend. We camped at a couple of sites but at no time were we more than 20 miles from home so could have been rescued should it all have gone horribly wrong.

If you want to go somewhere exotic where you've never been, where nobody speaks your language then maybe look for a guided and fully supported tour. If you're setting off from your front door it's easy to mount up and set off.

How much are you willing to spend?

Fully-guided, supported bike tours can start at £800 and go up to eye-watering levels. A fully supported tour with absolutely everything laid on in far flung places will not be cheap. There are differences not only in location, length of trip but quality of accommodation i.e. camping vs 5* hotels.

There will also be other aspects of "support" to consider, take your own bike or hire locally, will there be a mechanic or a guide attached to the group?

How much gear are you willing to carry?

If you're unsupported, you'll have to carry everything you need; clothes, wet weather gear, tools for bike repairs and maybe camping gear. It is potentially a lot of stuff that will all require packs and / or panniers. It is also the type of trip that requires extra preparation, as you need to practice packing and riding with that much stuff.

How long and how far do you want to ride?

The longer you want to go for, the more you'll need to take and the greater the likelihood that you'll encounter some adversity like bad weather or bike maintenance issues. In those situations, it might be an idea to have a bale out plan. This will be unlikely but if you're near a railway for instance, getting home might not be too much of an issue.

If lightly loaded, you'll cover more ground in any given amount of time, a relative beginner can easily cycle at about 12mph / 20kmh on the flat (depending on terrain of course), something to bear in mind.

What do I need to plan?

Will you need to make any transfers during the tour (ferry connections, border crossings etc)? What are the costs? When are services available? What is the prevailing wind direction; it's predominantly south to north in the UK for instance?

If heading somewhere far away be familiar with local laws and customs you might need to observe. Do you need any visas or immunisations; is your passport still in date? Is where you're going safe? Check travel advice on the Foreign and Commonwealth Office website (fco.gov.uk).

Don't forget you might also want some days off the bike.

The amount of planning depends on a number of things; length of trip, location, the degree of support and maybe time of year amongst others.

If travelling at a busy time of year or on a tight schedule you might want to book some or all of your accommodation. For instance, southern Europe is completely rammed with holiday makers in the summer, especially August when many Europeans take holiday. I've been turned away from campsites in southern France in June as they were full. In

21

addition, despite the weather usually being excellent for cycling, France tends to start shutting for the winter in mid September. Schedule reservations carefully, being conservative with the distances you might cover. Remember laden bikes go slower and unfamiliar areas can throw up difficult terrain, you also want time to stop and have a look around or maybe a long lunch so don't try and cram too much in too soon. Have contingency for bad weather and mechanical issues or maybe you'll see a turn-off you fancy taking.

But one of the best things about touring is the freewheeling nature of it all, so try to be as flexible as your itinerary will allow and you are comfortable with.

If you think you can get away with route planning on a day to day basis, do so, many people do. Booking places to stay in the morning for that evening or just turning up on spec can work depending on where you are. Remember though, the more remote the place, the fewer places there will be to stay.

In 2013, a group of us cycled the Southern Black Forest Cycle Route (*Südschwarzwald-Radweg*); we camped taking a list of campsites with us. Apart from one day where the campsite on our list had closed five years previously we were fine. As we were wondering where to camp that night, a guest house owner offered us beds at bargain prices, an excellent outcome.

Where to stay shouldn't become a huge issue, you don't want to spend all day worrying that you won't find a bed at your destination. One compromise is to follow a vague itinerary and book ahead, a day or two in advance, while on the road.

In 2019, I cycled solo along the Hebridean Way. As places to stay can be few and far between, I opted to stay in guest houses rather than camp (wild camping is allowed in most of Scotland), so booked all accommodation prior to leaving home. This meant I had a target for each day and indeed for the week as I had to meet my return transport at an agreed time and place.

What's your priority?

Is it getting as many miles under your belt or is it seeing stuff along the way at a comfortable 12mph? If you decide on a guided tour, know what your priority is before you pick one.

Some focus on low mileage on the bike to give you a chance to do other sightseeing for the bulk of the day. Others are very ride-focused, so you'll be on the bike for the majority of the day. There are culinary or wine tasting tours where eating and drinking plays as large a role as bike riding.

🚲 🚲 🚲

Do I enjoy my own company; am I better off in a group?

During a long ride, you get to know yourself really well. Even if you are riding with other people, cycling can involve long stretches of time when there really is nothing to do but pedal, watch the world go by and deal with being by yourself. There can be times when this is very boring! You can have too much of the forests of western France in temperatures of 33C believe me!

If you are planning on going solo, you will be spending large amounts of time alone, with very little in the way of external stimulation to distract you. Pedalling becomes automatic after a while and ceases to be a distraction.

Don't expect every day to pass like you're riding through an area of outstanding natural beauty, change can be gradual;

24

🚲

there can be a lot of nothing between places. There are some lovely beaches cycling south along the west coast of France but you can have enough of a good thing after many hours!

If you're in a group, listen to the advice the more experienced person might give you, but feel free to make your point obviously! Tell someone if you're in pain or tired or just fancy a break.

Take turns riding at the head or the group or into the wind while chatting to your buddies. If it's windy or a long day in the saddle is planned, consider "drafting" where you ride in the slipstream of another bike. A rider can save about 15% effort compared with the front rider, take it in turns so all benefit.

I've been asked if I get lonely when cycling solo. No is the answer, I've only ever been away solo for 7 days maximum and I'm more than comfortable in my own company. It's easy enough to find people to talk to if you feel the need, during the day you're interacting with many people, in your B&B, in shops and with other cyclists who are usually up for a chat. I've found people will often start talking to me if they see me with a fully laden bike, interested in what I'm doing, where I've been, where I'm going, why I'm doing it etc.

Cycling in a group or a pair is different as you tend to be more insular in many ways, concentrating on the group, chatting while you cycle. Make sure you pick your touring partner(s) wisely as they could have a big impact on the success or failure of your trip. Pick the right person to travel with on your bike tour and you'll come home with wonderful memories, pick the wrong touring partner and your bike tour could be doomed from the very beginning. We tend to tour as a 5 or fewer if someone is indisposed and have resisted requests for others to join.

Don't wait, while it would be good to have someone join you on your bike tour, don't wait around for other people. If you wait for others, you might be waiting for the rest of your life.

How uncomfortable could I be?

You will be riding a bicycle and spending most of your time away from shelter. You won't always be able to escape inclement weather, sun, or steep hills.

I've sheltered from rain in bus shelters, under trees, found an excuse to stop before a hill to check out something rather than

26

cycle up it and spent time in a Lidl near Montpellier hanging about near the frozen food section cooling down while it was touching 40C outside. This was until the security guard took a close interest in what a bedraggled group of British cyclists were doing.

There could be pain and discomfort, namely a sore backside or thighs, calves, wrists, neck, shoulders. These are perfectly manageable with training before the trip and / or frequent coffee and cake stops (not that I'm obsessed you understand!).

Can I solve my own problems?

Things can and maybe will go wrong, hopefully mostly trivial things. Small mechanical issues (see later for which tools to carry) such as punctures or a broken or lost piece of kit can happen. Carrying spares is encouraged but there is a limit of course.

Things outside your control can happen i.e. the nonexistent campsite above. In 2018 we were at Hamburg airport ready to fly home to Bristol when the flight was cancelled as the airline had gone bust. Nothing we could do about it so we negotiated with the check in guy for a bed for the night, a substantial food allowance and repatriation the next day.

The ability to think on your feet is key and if in a group, ensure you can come to an agreement quickly and sensibly. In our group of 5 there's always a majority but it's important to agree and respect the views of the others (even if they're not right!). If cycling solo then it's all down to you.

One of the appeals of a package holiday; which I've taken on a number of occasions, is the near-complete removal of unpredictability. If you're that way inclined then maybe an organised trip is the way to go for you. This won't eliminate issues but it does mean there's someone around to fix it or help sort it out for you.

Even organising a trip yourself, predictability can be in built in terms of miles per day, where to spend the night, carrying a list of bike shops, places to see etc. This certainly minimises the chance of something going wrong but can never eradicate it. Who plans for an airline going bust?

Why on earth are you doing this?

You will be asked why you are doing this trip or why you did that trip. Cyclists will want to know all the details; others will feign an interest to a greater or lesser extent. A couple of friends of ours were fascinated by the Black Forest trip mentioned earlier, so much so they borrowed our maps, guide book and notes and recreated it almost pedal stroke for pedal stroke. They decided to book no accommodation though (camping isn't for them) and came unstuck one night but met someone in a bar who offered them a bed for the night – pure luck.

Non cyclists may need some persuasion, some will not get it at all, I mean why cycle when there's a perfectly good train or road network?

How young and fit do I need to be?

There is no upper age limit for cycle touring. I've met people in their 60s and 70s (mainly in Germany bizarrely) on two wheels. Of course you should be physically active and robust, but the fitness level required depends on the terrain and how far you plan to pedal each day. Electric bikes are more and more popular; the Germans were all on electric bikes for instance.

If your daily aim is to ride 100km in mountains on your own, you should be comfortable riding 130km in a day before you set off; if you're going to meander along a river for 50km in a supported group taking in a large lunch, you'll be fit enough if you commute a couple of miles each way to work by bike. Sore nether regions are the most common physical complaints of non-cyclists: avoid this by spending time on your bike before the trip.

Whilst a good level of general fitness is encouraged, you may walk frequently for instance, the only way to train for a cycling trip is to cycle.

Do I need to be a bike maintenance expert?

No, not really. Before heading off on your own you should aim to be able to complete some basic tasks i.e. change inner tubes and repair punctures and if you're feeling very confident be able to replace a chain link and maybe adjust derailleurs and brakes.

If you are going on a long distance cycling tour, it would be beneficial to know how to complete more complex tasks such as spoke replacement, how to remove the rear cassette, change cables etc.

Some people choose to attend a bicycle maintenance class to acquire this knowledge. Others, including myself, pick it up as they go along over time and use YouTube frequently.

Maybe ask your local bike shop if you can volunteer and pick up tips along the way.

Don't be afraid to tinker with your own bike, bikes are inherently simple machines but don't do this late at night the day before you start your trip!

You can take all the tools, but if you don't know how to use them, they are dead weight. Knowledge, on the other hand, weighs nothing.

YouTube is full of good videos and there are many places in the UK which offer basic bike maintenance courses. If you're in a group, there may be someone willing and able to do these things so you don't have to.

Should I take my own bike or hire one locally?

Unless you're starting your tour in a recognised cycling area which is far from home, take your own bike as you'll be used to riding it. If you ride it regularly and you've had it serviced, it might be in better condition than a hire bike.

Ok there's a lot to unpack here, hopefully the next few sections will help put some context behind these questions.

🚲

Where and when should I go?

The river Loire looking fine (2012).

That's a question! The beauty of cycle touring is you can go anywhere at any time – in theory.

There are few things to consider of course, for instance, there's little point in travelling two days each way to get you and your gear there and back for (say) three days on the road. Also, you may not wish to tour the highlands of Scotland (no matter how beautiful they may be) in the middle of January.

Assuming you are thinking of your first or nearly first tour, start small; a long weekend and maybe cycle from home, stick to traffic free routes or minor roads and take a train back (or vice versa).

🚲 🚲 🚲

I live in Bristol which is well served with bike paths and ways of leaving the city. Bristol is on the junction of two main railway lines going west to south Wales, east to Bath, Reading and London, north to Gloucester and the midlands and south to Weston-super-Mare, Taunton and Cornwall. Bristol is also well served by National Cycle Network (NCN) routes with its creator, Sustrans, having its HQ in the city. NCN route 4 goes east west from London to south west Wales through Bristol and NCN route 3 from Lands End to Bristol along with other, more regional routes. In recent years, Sustrans have packaged and promoted routes or circuits i.e. Coast to Coast, Coast and Castles, the Hebridean Way etc. This is in an effort to encourage tourers to complete a route such as the Great Western Way rather than cycle 170 miles along route 4 from Bristol to London. Not all of the named routes exclusively use the Sustrans network;

🚲

there could be sections on busier roads for instance. Sustrans are introducing red squares on their blue signs signifying if the entire route is on the NCN.

Wherever you live, have a look at possible routes (sustrans.org.uk) and ways of getting to the start and home from the finish. It may be you feel confident enough to start your tour right outside your front door but cycling across a large, busy city isn't for everyone. I'll discuss these topics in more detail later.

European countries are similar in that there are a number of way marked cycle paths along the lines of the UK's Sustrans NCN routes. France and Spain have local "green way" routes along canals, old railway tracks and minor roads (Voie Verte and Vías Verdes respectively). Other European countries have way-marked routes; Germany especially is keen on river routes Elbe, Weser, Rhine etc amongst many others.

Additionally there are a number of Trans European routes created by Eurovelo (en.eurovelo.com). EuroVelo routes 1 (Atlantic Coast route), 12 (North Sea Cycle Route which also shares space with NCN route 1 and Coast and Castles) and 2 (Capitals route) are all in part on UK soil.

The point is, there is a great deal of choice, possibly too much! Indeed, when my touring friends and I start discussing our next trip, most of the time spent is agreeing where to go, once that's done, the rest is usually fairly straightforward.

∞ ∞ ∞

If you're starting small, this is likely to mean a trip in the UK but a few days in Europe is not necessarily out of the question; it depends on how adventurous you feel.

Settle on a route with good scenery, easy to navigate on a bike with suitable terrain and places to stop, buy supplies and stay the night.

You may be limited by the season or climate or you may have a specific timeframe in which to ride so investigate options based on that. If travelling in a group, the availability of the others is a factor which will need to be taken into consideration.

The UK has so many potential cycle routes, maybe consider the parts of the country which you've never visited. In the last couple of years, I've cycled solo in two areas in the UK I'd never previously visited, The Outer Hebrides and Northumberland and the Scottish borders.

If it's your very first time and you're feeling slightly apprehensive, consider a supported / guided and semi-guided tour with cycling experts who can help you get the most out of your trip.

What about the bike?

The Trek (minus bar ends) in Brittany (2017).

As long as you're comfortable on the bike i.e. it fits and you can handle it, in theory, any bike could be used for touring. It doesn't have to be an £8,000 carbon fibre road bike (but why would you want to tour on such a machine?), it could be a clunker. Tom Allen (tomsbiketrip.com) has toured on a "scrapyard bike" with the entire set up just over £25, a nice experiment but not for everybody!

Tim Moore is the king of wacky bike touring, in 2014, he released *Gironimo! Riding the Very Terrible 1914 Tour of Italy*, which recounts his 2012 recreation of the difficult 1914 Giro d'Italia. For the recreation he used a period bicycle and wore a reproduction period costume mostly made of wool. In *The Cyclist Who Went Out in the Cold: Adventures Along the Iron Curtain Trail* he tackled the 9,000km route of the old Iron Curtain on a tiny-wheeled, two-geared East German shopping bike. Both well worth reading.

If you have a bike, why not use that for your first trip? However, many keen cyclists will not need much of an excuse to buy a new machine. Unless you have unlimited funds and can buy a bike for every conceivable occasion, compromises will have to be made. It's likely you'll end up with a bike which will perform OK over many types of terrain but will not excel at any.

There are different types of bike, like anything they have pros and cons but it's recommended that you buy a bike for the kind of activity you want it for although if you want to buy a bike just because you like the way it looks, that's fine too!

Do you want a bike mostly for commuting? Do you want a versatile bike that can handle both tarmac and dirt tracks? Do you want to dress head-to-toe in Lycra and attempt the land speed record?

Many people who are new to cycling often opt for a mountain bike, purely because it somehow sounds like the most familiar. However, there's really no need to buy a mountain bike unless you want to go mountain biking as they're not that suited for road cycling.

🚲 🚲 🚲

Whilst browsing in a second hand shop I found a copy of "Cycling Science – how rider and machine work together" by Max Glaskin. Max runs through all sorts of science concerned with cycling such as forces acting on the rider and bike, how bikes stay upright, frame shape, power output (cycling is >98% energy efficient) and which muscles are used amongst other very science-based facts.

He notes while most bicycles are the same basic design, there are many variations on design and component specifications which can produce large differences in form and function.

Some designs are conceived to be efficient for a single purpose (a track bike for instance) while others can cross more than one boundary but with differing levels of performance in each different scenario.

39

🚲

Although the edges can become blurred, the common bike types include:

Touring bike.

Touring bikes are capable of carrying heavy loads and can be ridden comfortably over long distances with long days in the saddle. A typical touring bike has a longer wheelbase for stability and heel clearance, frame fittings for front and rear pannier racks, additional water bottle mounts (for cages), frame fittings for front and rear mudguards, a broader range of gearing to cope with the increased weight and touring tyres which are slightly wider than a fast road bike's to provide more comfort on poor surfaces. The frame is likely to be steel which, although can be heavier than alloy, is stable and can be welded easily should the worse happen a long way from home.

Road bike.

As the name suggests, road bikes are designed to ride on good road surfaces making road cycling as efficient as possible and because of that they perform terribly if at all on a mountain dirt track. Road bikes are designed to help cyclists get the most out of the road, including the particular geometry (i.e. frame shape) of the bike with narrow tyres and lightweight components. They always have very skinny tyres, drop handlebars (handlebars which curve back down underneath themselves) and a high gear ratio (set up to favour higher gears for speed).

Mountain bike.

Designed for off-road trails, meaning they're chunkier, have knobbly tyres and a frame geometry which makes them better suited for uneven terrain. They have a wide range of gears to help you get up and over mountains or across fields. Some have front suspension but are rigid at the back (hardtail), some have front and rear suspension for cushioning jumps and drops (full suspension), others have neither. Mountain bikes are not recommended for going fast on tarmac roads, cycling long distances, or commuting around town. It might be worth locking any suspension if using on road to save energy and also swap knobbly tyres for slicker ones.

Hybrid / commuter bikes.

These are a mixture between road bikes and mountain bikes and are usually a compromise. They are versatile and can

41

cope with a bit of everything but do not excel in any one thing. Hybrid bikes have flat handlebars instead of drop handlebars. Some models have front suspension and are designed with versatility and comfort in mind. They have the more comfortable geometry of mountain bikes but with slicker, narrower tyres.

Cyclocross (or cross) and gravel bikes.

Recently a new type of bike has appeared on the market – a gravel bike / adventure bike. A gravel bike is a lightweight hybrid bike which has wider but moderately smooth tyres and disc brakes.

They are similar in that both have drop handlebars. Cross bikes follow the tradition of road cyclists in the olden days, who would swap their slick road tyres for knobblier tyres and continue to train during the winter months. Gravel bikes are essentially road bikes designed to tackle a variety of surfaces, carry additional gear and are suitable for all-day riding on tracks or poor quality trails. A cyclocross bike is a specific form of drop-bar bike which is built to tackle the popular racing discipline of cyclocross held on muddy or sandy surfaces.

⚷

Folding bikes.

The Brompton brand is very much the market leader. Folding bikes are designed to fold up into a compact size so that they can be easily stored, or used to cycle to the station and fold up on arrival. They also fit neatly into a car boot or other small spaces. The small wheels (16 – 20inch) with a more upright geometry means they can be twitchy and tricky to handle in some circumstances.

Others.

These include recumbent (adopting a more prone position), good for those with back problems and can be more efficient but you are low down (but not great in traffic) and luggage carrying capacity isn't great. Tandems, two-seater bikes, a very efficient way of pedalling but being larger, they are more difficult to transport. Both tandem and recumbent come in road, hybrid and mountain versions. Fat bikes or snow bikes are off-road bikes with oversized tyres, typically 97mm or larger and rims 55mm or wider, designed for low pressure to allow riding on soft, unstable terrain, such as snow, sand, bogs and mud.

I'm sure I've captured the main types, quite a list as can be seen and I'm sure I've seen examples of all types on my travels including someone who chose to ride a fat bike the entire length of the Outer Hebrides "for the challenge". Too much like hard work if you ask me!

🚲 🚲 🚲

Hopefully the list of bike types isn't too bewildering, for a short tour, a hybrid bike is probably where you should start (unless you already have a bike you wish to use).

Bikes are essentially the same, two wheels, tyres, handle bars etc etc but when choosing a bike it's worth thinking a little more about the various major parts.

🚲 🚲 🚲

Tyres.

Depending on the type, your bicycle will have fat or thin, smooth or knobbly tyres. Most road bikes and touring bikes have thinner tires, while mountain bikes have bigger, fatter tyres.

🚲

Tyres are measured by diameter in mm ranging from skinny 23mm tyres on a road bike to 30-40mm on a touring bike and even larger on mountain bikes.

Each type of tyre has been adapted for the surfaces they are to be used on. Road tyres are inflated to 100 or even 120 PSI (pounds per square inch). A firm thin tyre on the road won't flatten much. The less the tyre flattens out on the bottom, the less surface area is in contact with the road. Less contact in this case means less friction and more speed. This is why keeping tyres properly inflated is important.

Wide and fat mountain bike tyres flatten out more on a hard asphalt surface and on a dirt trail, a mountain bike tyre "floats" on top of the rough surface while a thin road tyre would cut into the ground. They are typically inflated to between 30 and 40 PSI.

The flattening causes "rolling resistance"; this is how much energy is lost to the road as a wheel moves forward. Tyres with low pressure traveling on soft ground tend to have higher rolling resistance. This one of the major reasons why road racing is a faster sport then mountain biking.

Rough or knobbly treads grip dirt trails better, but create greater friction on smooth roads. Smooth tyres grip smooth roads better, with less resistance, but slip on dirt trails.

Handlebar types; drop or flat?

Drop bars give you more hand positions, an aerodynamic advantage, are better for climbing hills, can fit through more narrow spots in traffic and you can cover more ground faster.

On the other hand, parts are more expensive; the brake levers are not as easily accessible while riding; they don't offer as much control as flat bars; changing brake or shifter cables can be more difficult; there is less capacity to mount items to the handle bars and visibility can be poor with drop bars. Also, spending a long time with a bent back can lead to backache and it's not so easy to appreciate the (hopefully) wonderful scenery around you.

My choice would be flat bars as they give you much better control; components are cheaper; changing cables is easy; the brake levers are easily accessible; there is plenty of space to mount everything you want on your handlebars; they are more comfortable; visibility is better and they are better for non-cyclists and new riders.

🚲

They are not perfect of course as flat bars offer only one hand position (but this can be rectified with bar ends); they are less aerodynamic and they require a wider gap to pass through.

My bikes in the 1970s all had drop bars because that was the thing in those days but now I have flat bars with bar ends on my touring bike. The bike I hired for my Hebridean trip was a high spec Dawes Ultra Galaxy with drop bars. I got used to it, it was very fast but very twitchy especially when descending in the rain from The Clisham (Scottish Gaelic: *An Cliseam*), the highest point of the Outer Hebrides. Only slightly scary at times!

There are other pros and cons for other bike components, without getting too technical (and I'm not sure I totally understand all of it!) you might want to research gear ratios, clipless vs clipped pedals, wheel sizes, disc brakes vs rim brakes, tube vs tubeless tyres, steel vs aluminum frames and Presta vs Schrader valves. I'm not convinced any of these are crucial for the novice tourist but if you get the bug then you may have more decisions to make.

Or just get your bike out of the garage and head off.

🚲

🚲 🚲 🚲

The e-bike debate.

Before we leave this topic, I'd like to address the sometimes thorny issue of electric bikes / e-bikes. Apart from a tandem, fat bike and recumbent (they may exist), I've seen electric versions of all of the above types, even an electric Brompton.

Some consider it cheating in that you're being assisted by an electric motor so how can this be cycling? But surely if it means someone is able to get out on a bike where (maybe due to a medical condition or age) they could not, what's the problem? I've met many electric bike tourists, the Germans mentioned before and a fellow tourist on the Hebridean Way, he was 70, had cycled for years but age and a few health issues had caught up with him so he had adopted electric and couldn't get enough of it.

For an e-bike to be legal in the UK, the rider must be at least 14 years old and the bike restricted to a maximum speed of 15mph. Also, it cannot provide power unless you are pedalling, otherwise, it would be an electric motorbike and require insurance and registration.

48

🚲

They are expensive; hopefully the price will drop and heavier due to the battery pack and motor. Always check the maximum range as some can be as low as 20 miles. It's also very important to consider where you can charge it each night so camping; especially wild camping might not be an option. E-bikes are heavy so are difficult to pedal if the battery runs flat so be sure you don't exceed the limit and / or can charge easily.

They're a great option if you have concerns about your fitness level or if you're travelling with a group with different fitness or riding levels. If you have an injury or are recovering from an injury which makes riding a non assisted bike difficult then an e-bike might be for you.

Think about an e-bike if you're worried about distance or climbs or if you want to save your breath to hold a conversation during the tour. In very simple terms an e-bike works by adding "oomph" when you pedal. Sensors detect when you are pedalling and the e-bike then supplies extra power via a motor either through the wheels the crank.

Daily distance should play a part in your decision making. For instance, 40km could be "only" about 3 hours on your bike.

🚲

If this is much more than you're used to, you might want to consider an e-bike to help your legs.

🚲 🚲 🚲

The gender difference.

Men and women are different and so, in many cases are their bikes. The big differences are frame dimensions and the main contact points; the handlebars and saddle.

Women's frames (step through frames) historically don't have a crossbar. This was more to do with women not having to lift a leg and expose an ankle and also assist when wearing long skirts. Women's frames are now sold minus a crossbar due to convention rather than science.

Bike frames are triangles, as the triangle is inherently strong. A step through frame doesn't have a cross bar which can mean the frame is less stiff and not as strong. This is often corrected using extra or larger tubing making the bike heavier. One of my five regular cyclist friends is female and always opts for a bike with a cross bar.

🚲

On average, women are 15% lighter and 8% shorter than men (Max Glaskin) so women's frames should be smaller and be in different proportions than those for men.

Women's saddles tend to be wider and slightly shorter than men's due to the different anatomy.

However, if the bike fits and suits you then go for it.

My current bike of choice for touring is an aging, (vintage 2012) Trek 7.3 hybrid. It's been along the Loire valley, various other excursions into France and along the Coast and Castles route in the north east of England. For many years it was also my commuting bike but age and worn out parts finally caught up with it so I put it through a major rebuild, possibly the only original parts now are frame, mudguards and rear pannier rack. All being well, it will be off touring again in 2021. The point is, the bike suits my needs and I'm very comfortable riding it and keeping it running is cheaper than shelling out for a new machine, although I did buy a new commuter to take the pressure off the old Trek.

🚲 🚲 🚲

🚲

Whichever bike is used, it's worth taking time to ensure it is set up properly for you and configured for carrying the rider and all the touring stuff. As in all things, YouTube is packed with information on how to do everything to your bike, I'm not going to go into long boring detail on how to do stuff here, rather point out areas which might be worth looking at again. Having a bike that fits you properly is probably the most crucial thing to look for. A bike that is not the right fit for you may start to give you pain in your hands, back, shoulders, etc. in no time, especially if you are doing 50+ miles a day. A local bicycle shop (LBS) can do a full bike fit for a cost and a quick assessment in about 5 minutes (possibly free) but there are some fairly simple things which you can attempt yourself.

A bike fit will check everything from the height of your seat post to the length of your stem. This means you will be able to ride with your whole body; riding strongly and remaining comfortable while doing so. Almost any bike can be used for touring (depending on the length and severity of the trip) but you need to be comfortable on whichever bike you're on, that's the most important part. If you can get a touring bike, they hold the advantages of being much stronger and better

🚲

balancing the extra weight you're carrying – making riding a loaded bike more manageable.

🚲 🚲 🚲

Here are a few things you might want to think about checking for yourself.

Saddle and saddle height.

The first thing I did when I bought the Trek was to swap the factory saddle for a Brooks B17 leather saddle. After a few miles, the leather moulds to your posterior and is very comfortable.

Saddle-fit is very personal but is dictated by the spacing of your sit-bones (ischial tuberosities), this distance must be measured.

Make sure your saddle is at the correct height. Saddle height is important, you need to be comfortable when riding, enabling you to ride longer and to push harder. Getting the height right will also help prevent injury; compression injuries from having it too low and over-stretching issues from having it too high. Also ensure the tilt of the saddle is correct so

🚲

your weight is transferred to the saddle through your sit-bones.

One easy to find a good saddle height is the heel-to pedal method and while this doesn't take into account all of the elements that can affect saddle height, it does a job.

The heel-to-pedal method involves sitting on the bike, placing your heel on the pedal then pedal backwards to reach the six o'clock position. Your knee should now completely straight. If your knee is still bent you need to increase the height, adjusting in small increments each time and if your heel loses contact with the pedal then you need to lower the saddle.

You should be able to stay sitting on the saddle when stationary with the balls of your feet in contact with the ground.

Moving the saddle forwards or backwards along the rails is another important consideration when adjusting your saddle and should be considered once you've established your saddle height. The ideal position is to have your knee directly above the pedal spindle (known as the Knee Over Pedal

Spindle, or KOPS, rule) when the crank arm is in the three o'clock position.

If you're going for a professional bike fit, they will consider other items such as crank length and reach which all affect saddle height and position.

Make any adjustments to your position gradually, this will enable you to fine-tune your position and isolate what impact any change has on your comfort and efficiency.

Some cyclists use a gel saddle cover. I'm not convinced about these, especially for long distance cycling. Gel saddle covers tend to increase the contact area, increase movement in the saddle and increase heat, none of which are positive over an extended period of time on the bike. If you have a properly fitting saddle that has been well adjusted there shouldn't be a need for a gel seat cover as your nether regions will be happy. Your money might be better spent on a good quality padded pair of riding shorts.

🚲 🚲 🚲

🚲

Handlebars.

The different types of handlebars have pros and cons as mentioned above so make your choice between aerodynamic (drop) over comfort and stability (straight).

Touring is usually about long days in the saddle so comfort is paramount. Don't be afraid of raising your handlebars a little and making your position on the bike more upright. Add bar-end extensions to flat bars to give a variety of hand positions. Some tourists even attach aerodynamic tri-bars to their bikes but this will do you few favours in the stability department.

🚲 🚲 🚲

Handlebar reach and height.

Reach is the distance from the saddle to the handlebars. To adjust reach move your saddle forwards or backwards on the sliders under it or by changing the stem on the bike to either a shorter or longer one.

How do you know what the correct reach position is? It's mostly personal preference. A longer reach is a more aggressive position that is typical for a racing setup. Cycle touring is all about comfort so a slightly more upright

🚲

position is best but not too upright as this will cause more pressure to be put the sit bones. It will be obvious if the reach is too long as you'll feel stretched out and you'll feel squished up if the reach is too short.

Lower handlebars are associated with setups which are more focused on speed. As we are focused on comfort, a medium to higher handlebar height is advisable. This will put less pressure on your wrists. It should also help to avoid upper back and neck pain that sometimes occurs on cycle touring rides. The key is to have a variety of hand positions available to prevent pain or numbing of the hands.

🚲 🚲 🚲

Braze-ons for accessories.

If your bike does not come fitted with mudguards (fenders for our American friends) and racks it's worth thinking about them. Mudguards will help to keep you dry in the wet and racks will give you a place to strap your panniers and other stuff. To add these accessories though, your bike is going to need to have the bolt holes (braze-ons) to attach them with. Fixings for a bottle cage or two are highly recommended. Cycling in hot weather will result in the need for frequent

🚲

drinks from your bottle or Bidon (a container for water or other liquids, particularly as used by cyclists - "never ride with an empty Bidon or a full bladder"). It's also possible to buy containers for tools or valuables which will fit into a bottle cage.

If your bike doesn't have mounts for racks, options are somewhat limited. Soft frame bags attach to handlebars, frames and seats and can fit a huge range of applications, though they require a lighter packing list. Racks and panniers can ferry extraordinary loads. You may also consider a hybrid setup utilizing a combo of racks and panniers and soft luggage to get the best of both worlds.

To lessen the weight carried on the bicycle, or increase luggage capacity, touring cyclists may use bicycle trailers. Touring with a trailer isn't really a different type of bicycle touring, using a trailer is simply another way of carrying your gear.

I've used a trailer; it's a good method of transporting stuff. We took a trip along the Canal du Midi, flying from Bristol to Toulouse then driving to a bike hire place. The bikes were excellent but we managed to lose something in translation when asking for panniers as the owner translated our request as "sacoche" or satchel; the word is derived from an old French word ("panier") meaning bread basket.

Consequently, all we were offered was a selection of very small bags. Our only option was to hire a couple of trailers from him. As in all things, there are many types of trailer on the market so shop around.

Brake levers and shifters position.

Once again YouTube will come to your aid but it's important to ensure the controls are in the optimum position so wrists are not kinked or over extended. Things to consider include position, angle and reach (the distance the brake lever sits away from the handle bar). If the lever is adjusted too far out you may find yourself extending your fingers to reach the brakes making for a slower reaction time when braking meaning thereby losing handling capability by loosening your grip on the handlebar. There are also disadvantages to having the levers too close, slower reaction time and cramp in your fingers from continuously contracting your finger muscles to maintain contact with the lever. Brake lever reach is easily changed using the adjustment knobs.

As for the bike itself, gears need to be quite low and have a decent spread and wheels must be strong. Lightweight wheels with thin tyres do not bear the weight of panniers well and given the extreme position, you're better steering clear of a pure racing machine altogether. If you will be riding up any hills at all you will want a bike with a double or triple chain ring (the front sprockets) to increase the number and range of available gears. Gear numbers are calculated by multiplying the number of front (1 – 3) with the number of rear (typically 6 – 9). My Trek has 3 X 8 = 24.

If using an off-road machine exclusively on tarmac, avoid those with heavy power-sapping rear suspension systems and make sure you fit slicker tyres. 28mm is probably about the thinnest tyre you'd want to tour with on any bike.

There are also metric, imperial and American wheel and tyre sizes which are not always interchangeable. If touring on your own bike in a faraway place, check which size is dominant in the local area should you need to buy replacement parts. A good summary can be found here: cyclinguk.org/cyclists-library/components/wheels-tyres/tyre-sizes.

The majority of tourers will have cantilever brakes rather than disc brakes. Cantilever brakes are effective (less so in the wet) and easy to maintain on the road. Discs do have superior stopping power, especially off road.

🚲 🚲 🚲

If all the above sounds horrendously complicated, your LBS will be pleased to help (if they're not, find another one!).

Of course, you need to make sure your bike is in the best possible nick before you leave so think about taking your machine to your LBS for a tune up. The absolute bare minimum is to have two working brakes, apart from that your bike can be a clunker but don't underestimate the benefit of a well-maintained bike. A £50 service is a lot cheaper than a brand-new bike or coping with a major failure at the roadside. Your local mechanic can also help you identify any upgrades and changes within your budget to help make your bike trip more comfortable.

🚲 🚲 🚲

Two more useful things to know are the comprehensive "M" bike safety check see britishcycling.org.uk for more details.

🚲

The "M" check is a full bike check which should be carried out monthly / 6-weekly. A simpler, daily check is the ABC check, A for air (tyres), B for brakes and C for chain i.e. running gear, an example, can be found here: somersetroadsafety.org/page/abc-checks/175.

Some great "how to" videos can be found on YouTube, especially Park Tool and Art's Cyclery.

I'd recommend watching the M-check video about a month before a trip and booking your bike into your LBS should anything need fixing and the ABC check a day or so before you set off.

Your wheels must run smoothly, check for side to side play in the hubs and missing or slack spokes.

Tyres must be in good condition with plenty of tread and no signs of weathering or cracking and inflated to the pressure recommended by the manufacturer (see tyre side wall).

Brakes must be effective (legally in the UK, a bike must have two working brakes), pedals must turn smoothly and gears change smoothly.

All nuts and bolts need to be tight and apply oil to the chain and gears and have a couple of short "shake down" rides.

Buying a bike.

It's possible to spend £££££s on a bike or comparatively little.

New, cheap bikes are cheap for a number of reasons, they could be heavy, inefficient and poorly assembled and may well develop a mechanical fault.

A very cheap bike is worth nothing secondhand. By contrast, a decent £300 bike could easily be sold on for £150 or more.

Really cheap bikes still have to pass safety standards, so you're unlikely to suffer, say, a broken frame but will have cheaper components and may not have been assembled as meticulously. More care and attention will thus be needed to keep such a machine on the road. This requires time (by a competent home mechanic) or money (at the bike shop).

The fact that cheap bikes may be a false economy doesn't mean you need to spend several thousand to get a good one. Diminishing returns kick in around £1,000 or twice that for an e-bike or full-suspension mountain bike. Dearer bikes are still better but by smaller increments. Whether those differences in performance are indispensable, desirable, or irrelevant will depend on how the bike is used.

Buying a bike which costs several hundred pounds or more is a big investment but could be a good investment as long as the bike is good match for you and your cycling.

Go to your LBS and they will happily steer you in your purchase as they want you to be a cyclist and to be a repeat customer. That means selling you not just any bike but the right bike. Tell them how much you're looking to spend and what you'll primarily be using the bike for and they'll talk you through your options taking note of your requirements.

Most shops will allow you to have a short test ride before purchase while some online shops will offer you a money-back trial period.

Whatever price the bike you choose, you can save money on it through a scheme such as Cyclescheme (as long as the shop and your employer are signed up). Cyclescheme savings are at least 25% which makes a £300 bike a £225 bike. Additionally, you'll pay in installments so there's no big hit to your bank account.

So, you already have a bike or have bought a brand new machine and are ready to go…..or maybe you haven't so an option is to hire.

Should I hire a bike?

The Trek on a bridge over the river Tweed (2020).

If you don't feel your bike is up to the job or you've decided to start your tour in a place where it would be tricky or expensive to take your own bike then maybe hiring is for you.

It's very possible to hire decent touring bikes or rather, bikes which will do a job. This could be because you don't have a suitable bike or transporting your own machine is a faff or expensive. Bikes are great but it can be a pain transporting them, taking your own bike is usually the best option from a comfort and familiarity point of view.

Personally, I've hired bikes in Hamburg, Frieburg, Oban (Scotland), Montpellier and in the west coast of France.

🚲 🚲 🚲

What should you ask?

There are many places offering bikes for hire, but it's important to remember your home is potentially hundreds of miles from the hire place so you can't pop in for a chat and maybe there could be a language barrier. For the avoidance of doubt, be clear on requirements, any decent hirer will have a comprehensive website, make sure you can see the types of bikes offered on the website and feed back the requirements in the form of pictures i.e. send an email with a picture of the bike you are wanting to hire.

You should be asked some questions about the hirers, height (usually in metres) being the key so a suitably sized bike can be found. If possible go to the hire place so if the chosen bike isn't acceptable, there should be a replacement on site.

🚲

Be clear on your requirements, state explicitly where you intend to take the bike. Hiring a bike in a big city for a few days might lead to a bike that's great for pottering about an urban environment but of little use carrying loads for 50km a day for a week.

Many European city bikes are the "sit up and beg" or Dutch style, fun to whizz around a city but not so great for touring.

Make sure you know what's included and what's excluded. Typically, locks and sufficient tools, pumps and spares are included but are lights or helmets an option? Are the bikes fitted with pannier racks and bottle cages? Typically, hire bikes don't come with bottle cages but do have the fixings. I've brought my own from home, either borrowing from another bike or buying a spare; £5 will buy you a decent cage or buy one while you're away. Again use pictures to be clear on requirements.

The mantra is "if you don't ask, you don't get".

🚲 🚲 🚲

What support does the hirer offer? Do they come out in the case of emergency for instance? In the west coast of France,

🚲

one of my friends had a major wheel failure and the hire company were with us within 90 minutes with a complete bike to replace the failed one, no quibbling.

Be clear on shop opening times, in Hamburg we had to go to another hire place as our first choice was closed on the day we intended to return.

Does the hirer deliver? We had three trips to western France around the Bordeaux area and used bikehiredirect.com, a franchise around the west and south west of France. On our first trip, they were more than happy to deliver the bikes to us at our campsite in La Rochelle and collect them a week later from Bordeaux railway station.

Check for hidden charges. Will you be asked to pay additional insurance (very rare) or could any damage be paid for from any existing cycle insurance? The Hamburg shop wanted us to take out their insurance against damage or theft which we were reluctant to do. In the end we paid, between 5 of us it wasn't a huge amount of money.

The Frieburg hire shop quoted 5 Euros for cleaning so we made sure we cleaned before returning but they felt more cleaning was needed so went ahead anyway. Not the end of the world but the holiday ended on a very small sour note. I'd definitely use them again however.

Could the shop store stuff while you're away? It's more cost effective to put any checked-in baggage in as few bags as possible. So far, all the hire places we've used have been happy to hang onto our empty hold bags while we were away, it's worth asking.

🚲 🚲 🚲

One thing to remember, if hiring in a country which drives on the right, the brakes will be the opposite way around – not a huge deal but it takes a couple of miles to get used to it. In the UK, the front brake is on the right, in Europe and the USA for instance, it's on the left. There are a few internet theories about this but my favourite reason is, ideally the cyclist should use both brakes to slow down and stop but if you can only use one, use the rear to prevent a face plant. Cycling on the left and indicating right means you can slow down with the rear brake and indicate at the same time thereby crossing the oncoming traffic under control.

If you are cycle touring with rented bikes it is crucial that you are assigned the correct size bike and have the appropriate

🚲

adjustments made, i.e. seat height, saddle position and handlebar reach and height before you leave the shop. All these issues can be sorted out by email or phone prior to the trip.

In addition to bike hire direct, other hirers we've used and would use again are:

- Frieburg; radstation-freiburg.de/mobilitaetsanbieter/freiburgbikes
- Montpellier; cyrpeo.fr
- Hamburg; hhcitycycles.de/en
- Oban; rustycycleshed.co.uk/wp
- Barra (Outer Hebrides); barrabikehire.co.uk

I've never used Barra Bikes but they come highly recommended from a group I met on the Outer Hebrides. Nick at the Rusty Cycle Shed can also deliver to Oban from his premises or is happy for you to leave your car with him.

How do I transport my bike?

Plenty of room for bikes on the local train into Berlin (2011).

Ok, you've decided to take your bike on your adventure, how on earth are you going to get it to the start and bring it home from the finish? I've taken my bike on trains, boats, planes and in and on my car – it's all possible given a bit of thought.

🚲 🚲 🚲

Planes.

There's an ever growing debate about whether flying is sustainable. Much as we might prefer to use other, less

🚲

polluting transport, the only practicable means of access in a sensible time frame to faraway places is likely to be flying.

It is possible to take your bike on a plane, do your homework as each airline has their own rules regarding cost, how the bike should be contained and availability of bike spaces.

Bikes are large, oddly shaped, fairly heavy items and when you fly with your bicycle, airline companies are likely going to charge you extra. Most categorise bikes as "sports goods" and place them in the hold with skis and golf clubs.

How much is charged depends on the airline (some do transport for free!), don't assume all are the same and if you're returning from your adventure on a different airline or from a different airport from the one you flew out on, it might be totally different so check and double check.

Larger bags are harder to load and require special handling by the ground crew so, in many cases a charge is considered fair. Smaller aircraft might not have room for bikes, one of the reasons we chose to hire bikes in Hamburg was the plane from Bristol was a small, executive jet-type, the best they could do was ensure our bikes reached us "within a few days" – not ideal.

73

Before your bike flies, it'll need to be covered or in a bag or box. Airlines typically prefer hard-shell cases or cardboard bike boxes, but soft cases can work provided there is ample padding. You'll have to remove the pedals and turn the handlebars through 90 degrees and slightly deflate the tyres. The main reason for covering the bike is to protect other baggage from any oil and dirt on the bike.

Make sure you have all the relevant tools for reassembling and a bike pump handy at your destination.

ڶڶڶ

A hard or soft bike case is fine but will need storing while away. I flew to Berlin, staying the first night in a small hotel near the airport. While booking, we agreed we could leave our bike cases with the hotel (for a small cost) while we were away.

Another option is to wrap the bike in polythene which can be carried on the tour or go to a local bike shop (or large white goods shop – washing machines, refrigerators etc) and obtain a cardboard box, use it to carry the bike on the plane then dispose of it at the other end. The risk here is finding an accommodating shop on the return journey. Cardboard bike boxes can be bought and I've heard some airlines do provide them but I have no detail on this. On our Loire trip, four of us went to Paris by ferry and train to meet the fifth who had arrived a couple of days earlier by plane, wrapping his bike in cardboard and disposing of it (the cardboard!) on arrival.

🚲 🚲 🚲

Although airlines differ in requirements, some of the more common requests include:

Wheels.

It's likely you will have to remove one or both wheels. Use a spare quick release or other 10cm piece of metal tube on the forks as a dummy axle to stop the forks being squashed together. My bike bag came with spacers but a local bike shop may have transit packing materials which might do the trick. My bag also has two fabric wheel bags.

Handlebars.

Turn the handlebars but consider twisting them downwards so the levers are sheltered – essential if you have dual controls (easy to break, hard to replace). Protect exposed

🚲

bar-end controls by pieces of PVC waste pipe jammed on the ends of the bars.

Bottles.

Strap bottles in their cages strapped to the frame with tape, to protect cages and save space in luggage. A pump may be attached likewise, but risk of theft if visible in poly bag or denting if metal.

Mudguard stays.

Those with plastic safety-release fittings can be easily broken so detach from dropouts and tether with tape.

The best way to protect the frame against scratching is lengths of foam pipe lagging; available from any DIY shop. Bubble wrap is good for components and if your bike has disc brakes it is advisable to remove the discs and pack them elsewhere, for example in the back of a pannier - but NOT the one you plan to carry into the cabin!

🚲 🚲 🚲

When the check-in staff go to place flight labels on the packed bike, either pierce the plastic so they can loop it around the top-tube (crossbar) or handlebar (closer to the

🚲

stem than the brake lever, so that stops it sliding off) or a wheel (if the gap between spokes is wide enough), or stick the entire long label on the RIGHT side of the packed bike. That's the side with all the sticking-out things: the gears, the removed front wheel, and the turned handlebars.

Different airlines have different rules about travelling with your bicycle. In spring 2017, Yellow Jersey Insurance compiled information about airlines and their different rules to help you decide which airline to use and how you will need to pack your bicycle - yellowjersey.co.uk/the-draft/bike-luggage-charges-infographic.

Ensure you check if it's possible to carry non bike stuff in the bag or box with the bike as airlines differ in policy, some airlines are clear that ONLY the bike may be in the box. If you pack it full of other heavy stuff and they catch you, you'll need to pay a fee.

Including other gear with the bike can save hassle and sometimes the extra cost of needing to check-in a second bag. Also sleeping bags, clothing, etc. can be useful as padding if the box is large.

Ⓐ

If it's not possible to include other gear in your bike box or bag, package the rest of your gear in a separate smaller cardboard box and check that as a second bag. Alternatively pack your gear in your panniers and check one or both (carry one as hand luggage). Another option is to tape panniers together back-to-back (to protect attachment points) and / or combine them in a large zippered bag or a cheap duffel bag that you can leave when you arrive or carry with you on the trip. We tend to use a larger bag to carry panniers and tents thereby checking in a couple of bags rather than five.

If you do put panniers in the hold, I'd recommend removing the strap if there is one and the clips or brackets used to attach to the rack, easy enough on my Altura bags. This is because they stick out so removing them reduces any risk of loss or damage.

Make sure all tools and sharp objects including tent pegs are in checked baggage. Bring extra tape in your carry-on in case an official asks to open your bag or box, or if a weak spot will show up as you drag it through the airport.

Don't forget you have to get to and from the airport with bike, touring gear and packing materials. Public transport may not be an option although some large airport buses may have enough room. As we managed to negotiate in Berlin, the hotel near the airport was very happy to assist, they came to meet us and transported us and our stuff to the hotel. Asking a friend or family member for a lift is often a good solution. Depending on your bike packing supplies, you may be able to pedal to the airport of course.

At both check in and arrival, your bike is likely to be received and returned at the Oversize Baggage area which may be separate from the other check in desks or baggage reclaim.

🚲 🚲 🚲

On arrival at your destination, the bike will need to be reassembled – I've seen this happening inside the airport terminal (I've seen travelers disassembling bikes in the airport prior to flying also).

We left reassembling to the next morning outside the Berlin hotel on the grass much to the amusement of passersby. One possible problem with this approach, in the unlikely event the bike is damaged or any items are missing, a claim

79

🚲

will need to be filed within just a few hours of picking up your luggage.

Hopefully you took it apart yourself so you know how this works! Doing a practice run or two at home first will help the process.

🚲 🚲 🚲

Trains.

It's possible, free (or at least very cheap) and mostly straightforward to take bikes on trains. I've taken bikes on trains in the UK and France and Germany. The difference between these countries and the UK is marked. The man in seat 61 (seat61.com/bike-by-train.htm) has some useful information as do the individual rail company's sites.

My impression is, in the UK, bikes seem to be a bit of a nuisance and are tolerated by the train companies rather than welcomed aboard. Booking is usually required but this doesn't always ensure your bike will get on the train if there's no room. I used to travel with my bike on the train regularly but haven't so much in recent times. I'd think carefully about a trip which requires a change from one train company to

🚲

another, the thought of being stranded far from home doesn't appeal.

My experiences with trains and bikes in Europe couldn't be more different. Bikes are positively encouraged with large, dedicated sections, indeed entire carriages set aside for transporting bikes. I've usually booked my bike on a specific train but there has always been plenty of room.

Fares are cheap compared to the UK. During the Loire valley trip I had to return home after about 10 days, cycled to the station at Tours and bought a ticket to Caen for a ferry to the UK, a 4 hour journey with bike for 30 Euros – bargain!

One thing to remember, the bike carriages may be at set points on the train so ensure you're standing in the correct area ready to load. It's common to have a train map on the platform showing the bike carriage(s) and where they will arrive. Try and sit near the bikes if possible. On the trip to the Elbe, we took a train from Berlin and had booked bike spaces. There was a special deal where we were offered a free upgrade to 1st class which of course we took. The trouble was 1st class was at the opposite end of the train from the bike carriage. All was going well until we realised we were pulling into our destination of Lutherstadt Wittenberg so had to leap nimbly from the train and hare its length, toting our panniers and ignoring the whistle signalling the train's departure. Luckily we managed to throw ourselves and bikes to the platform in time as the train pulled away under the scowling gaze of the German train manager. Disaster averted!

I've never come across a train company which doesn't allow bikes, check before travel but Eurostar does have very specific requirements including ensuring your bike is in a box. This can be the owner's or can be rented from Eurostar.

Local trains are usually better then the high speed (the French TGV for instance) for carrying bikes as far as number of spaces is concerned and the ability to just turn up and get on. You'll take longer to reach your destination but travelling by train is a great way to see the countryside.

🚲 🚲 🚲

Ferries.

Living on an island, travelling to another country means moving over water either flying or by ferry. My friends and I

🚲

have used ferry from Portsmouth to France on many occasions and I've travelled from Oban to the Outer Hebrides, a highly recommended method of transport. If you have time to spare and are not keen on taking a car or flying with a bike I'd recommend ferry and train.

Cross channel ferries I've used are LD Lines (now defunct), Brittany Ferries to France and Condor Ferries to Guernsey. Caledonian MacBrayne (CalMac) provides services to and from and inter island in the Outer Hebrides. All companies welcomed bikes on board, making it very easy to use their services. Small ferries such as those across major rivers such as the Elbe. Weser, Rhine and Garonne are, in my experience, all very bike friendly.

Bikes are occasionally free or cost a small amount with the owner embarking as a foot passenger. Bikes are loaded on first (walk your bike onto the ferry) and secured and typically off last.

Remember to arrive at check-in in good time as you will embark before most other vehicles. Also remember there's usually no access to your bike during the passage so take all the stuff you need after you've secured the bike. I usually

83

歷

leave one pannier on the bike with everything I need for the trip in another, saves lugging two bags around.

🚲 🚲 🚲

Delivery services.

I've never done this and I don't know anybody who has but parcel and delivery companies will deliver your bike. See bikedelivery.co.uk, parcelmonkey.co.uk/bikes and parcelforce.com/help-and-advice/sending/bicycle amongst others. There are more but all insist the bike is in a box, pedals removed etc. Parcelforce have a set of photos and videos showing how to do this.

It's an option if you can't get you and your bike somewhere or want to go somewhere first and start your bike ride a few days later where the bike will be waiting for you. I'd suggest booking a night in a guest house and have the bike delivered there if that's your option.

Using this method to return means you can ship the bike home and go somewhere on the way home.

🚲

Bike transport / cycle taxis.

There are companies which will collect you and your bike and transport to the nearest station or ferry terminal for instance.

I used one after my Outer Hebrides trip (HebShuttle). I was collected at the end and driven south to the ferry in Castlebay on the island of Barra and caught the ferry to return to Oban the next day.

A quick internet search will throw up similar services operating around John O'Groats. pedal-power.co.uk/transport offer similar services around cycling routes in northern England i.e. Coast to Coast, Hadrian's Way and Coast and Castles. This means it's possible to be returned to the start of your journey if you're ending somewhere inaccessible.

🚲 🚲 🚲

One method of moving you and your bikes to Europe is the coach company European Bike Express (bike-express.co.uk). I've no firsthand knowledge but they do have good reviews. They offer bike transport for you and your bike into Europe

🚲

from 14 UK points and 21 points in France and Spain by coach. The bike remains fully assembled but with the handlebars turned through 90 degrees.

Bike Express has three unique routes; Atlantic route A serves Western France while the Mediterranean routes Med A and Med A Express serve Central, Eastern and Southern France and Northern Spain.

🚲 🚲 🚲

Car.

Transporting by car is an option but I'd always advocate public transport where possible. Four people in a car with bikes may well be the cheapest option however.

The car will need to be left somewhere and retrieved post tour. I've heard of groups using two cars, leaving one at the start and one at the finish of the trip.

Parking can be scarce and / or expensive, that's true of Oban for instance. Options include staying in an hotel on the first night and negotiating to leave the vehicle there or finding a quiet side street with no parking restrictions. We've used the latter in Portsmouth prior to boarding a ferry. A residential

🚲

street which had a long wall near one end so we could park without inconveniencing residents. Within reason it's possible to park away from the start point, you are on bikes after all. Cycling to the ferry via a pub and chippy for an evening sailing was a great way to start a tour.

I've used a parking app; justpark.com where it's possible to pay to leave your vehicle on private property or in an hotel car park. Prior to catching a ferry in Portsmouth, I left my car on a private driveway in Gosport for about £15 for a week, cycled to the Gosport ferry to Portsmouth then to the cross channel terminal.

Remember, you will need to return to your parked vehicle post tour so that will need to be planned into the itinerary.

I've "toured" by car where we drove to a campsite near Bayeux and used the campsite as a base, cycling off for day trips from there.

What should I take with me?

The Lichfield tent in western France (2016).

The amount of equipment you need does not necessarily increase with the length of your travels; you will find you may need a similar amount for a weekend away as for a month in the saddle. Pack efficiently and realistically; what is the minimum you need to enjoy the way you want to tour?

Packing efficiently does not always mean cutting the amount of equipment, look to upgrade equipment with lighter, more packable and higher performing options.

There's a rule of thumb, lay out all your stuff then put 50% away. This couldn't be more relevant for cycle touring as you want to travel as lightly as possible and choosing what to take inevitably becomes a compromise.

If this is the preface to your first tour, it'll probably be a short tour so you won't need vast amounts of stuff. If you're not camping, even less and if supported, very little. A couple of panniers should do it.

Depending on distance, time away, climate, whether camping or not etc there are a number of categories and many items which I would consider essential and some nice to have. I have packing lists which I tweak every time I go away but are always useful as a start point. Within reason, never take anything you wouldn't get too upset about if it went missing or was damaged, exceptions being camera equipment etc but a cheap cycling top could be expendable. I had a cycling shirt pegged on the rear of my bike drying after being washed but it slipped and was caught in the wheel making a couple of large holes and big greasy marks. Annoying but I used it once more on the trip then binned it.

Remember, this is supposed to be fun not an ordeal so there is always room for the little luxuries, maybe a book or two or travel games or bars of your favourite chocolate for instance.

Although unlikely on a short trip, it's possible to ditch gear as you go. For instance, if you're travelling south, the weather (should!) get warmer so maybe you want to think about losing that extra fleece on route. A tatty old fleece may not be hard to let go, donate to a charity shop or think about mailing stuff back home. This is a common trick used by long distance cyclists, gear that's no longer needed including maps and books can be mailed home thereby freeing up space and lightening the load.

Clothing can be washed and dried on route; man-made is best for this. If the weather is warm, it can be draped over the bike while cycling and dries in no time. On our European jaunts we tend to wash kit as we go and dry either on the tent overnight or pegged onto parts of the bike the next day. I have a disturbing memory of one of my friends cycling into a

⑅

lovely French village with a pair of boxers fluttering from his brake cables, be careful what you expose and to whom!

🚲 🚲 🚲

Cycle Clothing.

A key category this, you are touring by bike so will need suitable gear to wear. The most important item of clothing for me has got to be padded shorts. Days in the saddle may result in some degree of irritation or discomfort. Use cycling specific Lycra and / or baggy shorts with a padded insert but don't wear everyday underwear beneath them. Take a minimum of two pairs (that applies to all cycling gear), washing and drying between uses, so you can step into clean shorts each day.

It's possible to pay a premium for cycling gear but as mentioned before, outlets such as Aldi and Lidl do have bargains as do many chain sports shops.

Similarly, other points of contact with the bike are worth paying special attention to. Shoes should be comfortable and fit well. If you normally use hard soled road cycling shoes, picking up a pair of off-road leisure or more touring

🚲

orientated shoes with a softer sole may make activity off-the-bike easier. Choose your style wisely and you may even get away wearing them with civvies.

A clean change of socks will be needed and while not everyone likes to wear gloves or track mitts on their bike, several successive long days of riding can take a surprising toll on your hands.

As for other items of clothing, what and how much you take depends on the nature of your trip and the conditions. At least one change of jersey or top should be packed while wet weather gear should never be overlooked even in the height of summer and always layer for warmth.

I do a bit of running and have a drawer full of free synthetic running tops ideal for cycling and they're mostly in bright colours. Check out your local charity shop but one word of caution, don't go for luminous green tops as bugs will be attracted to you and you'll have a swarm around you as soon as you stop. One advantage of taking cycling shirts is they have rear pockets for bits and bobs i.e. snacks.

The best clothes for bike touring are a personal choice but the items below should get you through all but super-extreme conditions, without taking unnecessary things.

Generally, make sure your clothes are, lightweight, fast drying, warm enough for your conditions but only as much as you need and (optionally) bright to keep you visible when cycling on public roads.

My essential items:

- Cycle touring shoes (either bespoke or a pair just for cycling with another for time off the bike)
- 2x Lycra padded shorts
- Over shorts
- 3x cycling socks
- 2x Cycle jersey / manmade t-shirts
- Waterproof Jacket
- Thin Gloves
- Cycling sunglasses
- Neck tube / Buff

I always take baggy, ventilated cycling shorts (Endura) to wear over my Lycra shorts. Firstly they have pockets to carry small, essential items but secondly (and more importantly!) a 64 year old man rocking up to a small bar in the French countryside dressed in a pair of tightly fitting Lycra shorts is not something I'd wish to see!

Breathable hiking socks do a great job and are harder-wearing than traditional cycling socks. They can keep you nice and warm in the winter but don't make your feet overheat in hotter conditions. I usually take running socks which do a good job.

Even warm regions can be cold at elevation or in windy conditions so maybe a thin top or gilet might be useful.

🚲 🚲 🚲

I always take a waterproof cycling jacket. I have a bright yellow Altura jacket which folds and rolls small. Unless you're 100% sure rain is not likely, you will need one in northern Europe. It's also useful if chilly as it's wind proof. Mine has under arm air vents which can be opened or closed. The only time I haven't taken one is in 2019 when we were touring around the Montpellier area in southern France and the weather was forecast to be the driest and hottest for years. It was, one day we cycled in 40+C, not much fun so we cut it short and swam in the sea. Cycling along the Elbe on another trip, we came into a big rain storm. One of my colleagues always packs lightly and had not brought a waterproof top. He improvised by finding a (clean) rubble

🚲

sack on a skip and cut holes in the top and sides for head and arms. There's always a way but I'm not sure the owner of our Gasthaus near Dresden was too impressed both with trying not to laugh at my friend and with me dripping all over the signing in book (I'd not bothered with my waterproof that day as it was warm so got soaked – skin dries quickly)!

No matter what you wear or don't wear - you will be wet when riding in the rain. All you can do is try and mitigate that or (if very warm), just embrace it and get wet! Wearing quick drying man made clothing will help you dry quickly.

One of my friends invested in a pair of rain legs (rainlegs.com). They are light (150g) and cover the front of your thighs while cycling in the rain. Worn around the waist, they unclip and roll down thereby covering the most exposed part of the legs and reducing condensation (sweaty legs from wearing waterproof trousers). He swears by them.

A neck tube / scarf / bandana / Buff can be used in cold weather over your face or over your head. They can actually be used for many things and work well in a variety of weather conditions including protecting your neck from the sun.

Cycling sunglasses stop the sun and bugs going in your eyes.

Nice to have (some may become essential depending on the weather forecast):

- Waterproof trousers
- thermal top / bottoms / microfleece
- Thick gloves
- Warm hat
- Insulated Jacket
- Gilet
- Cycling cap
- Overshoes
- Helmet
- Hi viz
- 2x Loose base layers
- Longsleeved mid-layer

Waterproof trousers will keep you dry but can be sweaty. Most times I let my legs get wet, they soon dry.

The need to wear a helmet is constantly being debated, there are arguments for and against, the internet is stuffed full of information with Chris Boardman particularly vocal on the subject. As an adult make up your own mind. The same is true for the wearing of hi viz. Whatever your stance on this, make sure you're familiar with the laws of the countries you plan to visit. For instance, hi viz is mandatory in Italy in some circumstances. Helmets are mandatory in some countries i.e. Argentina and some states in Australia and countries have differing rules for minors. Bizarrely, in Spain the wearing of helmets is mandatory if you're cycling on inter-urban routes except when going uphill or in hot weather. There's plenty of scope to bend rules here I think!

Personally I do wear a helmet when appropriate to do so but if you are run over by a truck, you're probably in big trouble and a helmet will not save you. If it's raining or you're in heavy traffic then consider it. If you're on an empty bike path in glorious sunshine then maybe not.

🚲 🚲 🚲

A hard-wearing and breathable jacket is key for colder climates; it'll keep you warm, dry and also work as a windbreaker. I use my rain jacket as a windbreaker.

Thermal layers i.e. mid and base layers should be considered depending on the weather. One rule of thumb is to start cycling when slightly chilly, you'll soon warm up but if you start cycling when too warm, you'll rapidly overheat. Baselayers are often more practical than cycling jerseys and considerably lighter. You can find cheap baselayers (less than

🚲

£10) and they can be worn casually or for hiking, with thicknesses to suit your conditions. Add them under jerseys for extra warmth. Ones with thumb holes on the sleeves can give extra warmth over the hand and knuckles which is good for cycling in cold conditions. A good lightweight fleece will keep you warm when it's not quite cold enough for bigger outer layers. Make sure it's quick-drying in case you get caught in a downpour!

If you take a hat, a simple beanie hat which wicks moisture and keeps you warm is a good investment. A cycling cap under your helmet will keep rain away from your eyes, shields you from the sun and restricts the heat loss from the head and the brim stops spray.

Overshoes are recommended if you're likely to be cycling in torrential rain but in many cases its fine to let your feet get wet, they'll soon dry.

I've heard ultra light tourers sometimes use women's nylon tights or stockings (cut, of course) as arm or leg warmers saving on long cycling trousers and wear them under trousers. Apparently they are useful as sun-screen for the arms and legs too; I leave this decision up to you!

🚲

🚲 🚲 🚲

Non cycling clothing / casual clothes / civvies.

Regardless of your plans, you'll want some sort of clean off-bike clothing to change into after riding. Go for function over fashion. During the summer, lightweight trousers or shorts, a t-shirt, a light sweater or fleece and flip-flops may well suffice. No matter how light you want to pack, it's good to take a few casual clothing options. This is useful if your gear gets wet or dirty whilst cycling so you can change into something warm and you might be eating out or going to a bar etc, it's not a great idea to go out in full on cycling gear!

Aim for your casual clothes to be warm, quick-drying and lightweight, if you're touring through cold conditions think about taking long-john-style thermal top and bottoms to sleep in.

My essential items:

- 2-3 t-shirts or casual shirts
- Trousers or jeans or shorts
- 1-2 pairs of casual socks
- 3-5 pairs of underwear (quick-dry)
- Cool-weather jacket or rain jacket
- Sandals / trainers / other shoes

99

🚲

Nice to have (some may become essential depending on the weather forecast):

- Extra layers and gloves for cooler season or climate (thin, thermal, water-resistant)
- Swimming trunks / Bathing suit
- Long sleeved top / baselayer
- Thermal top
- Arm and knee warmers?

🚲 🚲 🚲

Spares and tools.

Inner tube(s), tyre levers, pump, repair kit and a multi-tool are essentials, beyond that it depends on where you're going, your mechanical skills and how long you intend to be away for. Decent bike parts can be hard to find in very isolated areas but for most destinations it's pretty impractical and pointless to carry a whole bike's worth of spare bits around. In the unlikely event you do have a major failure; it's unlikely you will be far from a bike shop. One tip, if you've planned your route, include a list of bike shops with contact numbers should the worse happen.

All the recommended tools are affordable and easy to find but are important to have with you. Taking tools will help

🚲

keep a small problem a small problem if you deal with it early, rather than a major failure miles from civilisation.

If you're going to be touring from city to city then maybe you don't need lots of spares, don't worry about extra tyres and brake pads; you can easily pick them up along the way. I had a saddle break while cycling to the ferry in Portsmouth. On arrival in Le Havre we hopped on a train for a few stops to get us out of the industrial area. Leaving the station at our destination, I walked out of the station, into a lovely square full of cafes and a bike shop – perfect. On another trip, my friend somehow managed to snap his seat post just as we were cycling into Rouen, the bike was cyclable but he had to remember not to try and sit down! A group of local lads came to our aid, guiding us to a bike shop.

🚲 🚲 🚲

Other possible items to consider are brake and gear cables; a few spare links and a chain tool. Even if you don't know how to properly fit them, a few spare spokes (of the same sizes which are on your wheels) and a spoke key might be useful. A local bike shop should be able to assist.

🚲

Duct tape, insulating tape or superglue will be useful for all manner of sundry repairs.

The most useful tool of all, though, is probably a bit of cash or a credit card. Even if you can't get your bike repaired where you are, it'll help you move to somewhere you can.

There are some definite items which must be taken; others depend on (say) newness of bikes and likely proximity to bike shops.

Rather than buy a complete Allen key set, it may be easier to take just the keys needed, saving weight and space.

Having said all that, in many years of touring I've had a few punctures, one snapped chain and a broken saddle, both of the latter are highly unusual. It depends on how risk averse you are.

My essential items:

- 2x Bungee cords
- 3x Tyre levers
- Bike lock – D-lock with cable
- Headtorch
- Rechargeable bike lights
- Replacement inner tube and / or puncture repair kit
- Multi tool / Allen key set / screwdriver set

- Lightweight bike pump
- Zipties / cable ties
- Link extractor / chain breaker

Bike lights might be necessary if you're likely to cycle after dark; I have rechargeable ones which last for a long time on a charge. Another option is a headtorch but using one as a front light is not generally legal as lights must be fixed to the bike. A headtorch is useful if camping however.

I carry a spare tube and a puncture repair kit. It's quicker to change the tube and repair the puncture later at your leisure. Get good quality tyre levers, something to sand down the tyres, some chalk to mark them and good quality patches and glue. Glueless patches can be quicker but often don't last for as long as a patch and glue.

A small Allen key set and a small screwdriver set or multitool are cycle touring essentials – don't leave without them. Both are small, cheap and able to take most parts of a bike apart and put it back together.

Whilst it's good to save space, minipumps can take a while to fully inflate a tyre. A mid-sized one with a pressure gauge is a good choice. Make use of any pumps on cycle ways, these

🚲

are becoming more and more common and a bike shop will usually be happy to give you a free puff of air.

🚲 🚲 🚲

Zipties / cable ties are often stronger and more convenient to fit than some metal fittings, are cheap and can be found all over the world. I've used them for all sorts including re-fixing a rack when the screw fell out. They come in different sizes and are perfect for many running repairs.

Wrap duct tape around your seat post, you won't notice it's there and could find many uses for it. Duct tape is great for quick fixes, whether it's fixing leaks in your tent, holes in your panniers or holding your bike lights together. Insulating tape is another potential life saver.

Compression straps / bungee cords (to hold things on to the back of the bike) and / or string / thin rope are also invaluable. They can be used to strap anything from your camping tent, camping gear, plastic water bottles or even food to your panniers. I use them for strapping my wet washing to the top of my rack and a baguette ready for a picnic when in France.

🚲

I had a chain snap while touring, luckily I was only a couple of miles away from a bike shop and luckily it was downhill all the way. It was a simple fix with a link extractor / chain breaker and I've carried one ever since. Needless to say I've never used it!

Tools can be very heavy; look for small and light so you don't need to carry unnecessary weight. If you're touring in a group, discuss which tools etc you need and spread the load, you'll never need 6 multitools!

Nice to have:

- 2x adjustable spanner (wrench)
- Rag for dirty bike
- Pedal spanner (if having to remove pedals for transport)
- Pliers
- Small bottle of lube
- Tubeless tube sealant
- Spoke key
- Spare spokes
- Assorted screws and nuts
- Spare brake and / or gear cables
- Spare brake pads / shoes
- Universal Derailleur Hanger

Take two lightweight spanners so you can unscrew things with nuts and bolts on either side. Also, make sure they aren't too thick so you're able to remove (need a 15mm spanner for this).

A rag is useful to clean grease and dirt from the bike and also helps to keep parts clean if you're dismantling sections of your bike.

Spare fittings and bike parts; think about taking spare nuts, bolts and fittings in case anything falls off along the way and maybe spare brake cables and / or gear cables. If you're in relatively developed areas I don't think you really need to take more spares than this, but that's a personal choice. If you don't want to carry spares leave your cables long at the end and wind them into a loop. If your cable breaks then you can at least tie it until get you to the next bike shop.

🚲 🚲 🚲

Camping Gear.

It's very difficult to find camping equipment which is suitable for all conditions. When picking a tent and sleeping gear, think about where you're going, at what time of year and pick equipment suitable for it. You don't want to be stuck in

🚲

a thin, summer sleeping bag if you're going to be touring in a European winter.

Everyone wants lightweight cycle touring kit and your sleeping gear is an area where you can cut down. Tents, sleeping bags and camping mats can be very heavy so shop around.

It's better to invest in products which will last, skimp on everything else, make sure your sleeping and pannier setup is the best possible.

If you're planning to camp, you'll have more gear to fit onto your bike. If you're planning to camp for the majority of time away, go for it but it's not worth lugging camping gear for one night out of your 7 nights away.

🚲 🚲 🚲

My essential items:

- Tent
- Tent repair kit (usually sold with tent)
- A roll mat inflatable camping mat.
- Appropriately insulated sleeping bag
- 5 washing pegs
- Short section of washing line
- Camping cutlery set

🚲

- Steel camping mug
- Bowl / plate

Don't scrimp on the tent, it's going to be your home and will need to stand up to rain, wind and being put up and down many times. A small lightweight tent (1.5kg or less) is recommended, always go for a small 2 person rather than a 1 person, they're not much bigger when packed but you get extra space for you and your stuff in the tent. If you're sharing consider a 3 person tent for 2 etc.

I bought a new one for a trip along the Loire in 2012. As you might expect, there are almost too many to choose from. I spent ages measuring myself when prone and sitting to see if I could fit. It's been a good tent; a Lichfield Treklite. Prior to the very hot trip to Montpellier, I bought a cheap £10 two-man from Asda as all it had to do was provide cover; it's a throw-up-and-secure-with-a-couple-of-pegs type, an excellent purchase.

Have a look at ease of erection, does it have a flysheet and does it have a "porch" to leave some gear outside the tent at night?

🚲

Think about painting your tent pegs a bright colour or add some brightly coloured tape so they are easy to see when you pack up each day. I've spent time looking for lost pegs on a campsite, I've also found a few on my travels! Triple check your camping spot before you leave. The worst miles are heading back to pick up something you've forgotten.

🚲 🚲 🚲

Check the Hydrostatic head (now were getting technical!). This is the rating of the tent's waterproof coating (or PU). For instance, a Hydrostatic Head of 1,000 is the legal requirement to be able to call a tent waterproof, most start at 2,000. Any tent rated from 2,000 – 3,000 should cope with British rainfall. My Lichfield is rated at 3,000.

Most tents have these but a sewn in groundsheet will prevent anything crawling in or out and keep it free from drafts.

Check the dimensions, prior to buying my tent, I lay on the floor and worked out the dimensions of the tent around me, don't forget the height as you may want to sit up and move around.

109

🚲

Practice pitching your tent before you go and maybe sleep in it in the garden for a night or two. Arriving at a campsite and pitching your tent for the first time might not be a great idea, also make sure you can pack it all away properly.

🚲 🚲 🚲

A sleeping mat is essential; you could be camping on any surface. There are ridiculously lightweight camping mats available but they're very easy to puncture. I have a three quarter self inflating mat from Go Outdoors, cost about £15. Use a sleeping mat as a barrier between the cold ground, the sleeping bag and you. Whether it's a simple foam roll mat, a self-inflating mat or a blow up mattress, your night in the outdoors will be much more comfortable if you have something to sleep on.

🚲 🚲 🚲

Unless you're certain night temperatures will be high, a sleeping bag is a must. Shop around and get one which will cope with the lowest forecast temperature while you're away.

🚲

Think about where you are going, the kind of temperatures you will experience, which sleeping bag rating you will need and whether you will need to consider weight when carrying it for long periods of time. To help with this decision there is something called the "warmth to weight ratio". This is the effectiveness of the insulation and balancing it against weight.

For example, a down sleeping bag will be very warm and very light. If a bag uses synthetic insulation then it can still be as warm but it will need much more insulation to achieve the same temperature rating so it will not be as light. The two bags are as warm as each other, but the first has much better warmth to weight ratio.

Look at the "season rating"; this is the lowest temperature in which you should be able to have a comfortable night's sleep. It's recommended buying a sleeping bag which offers a comfort limit slightly lower than the temperature you are expecting to sleep in allowing for a couple of degrees as insurance, so you can sleep comfortably at the predicted outside temperatures.

Synthetic sleeping bags don't require a great deal of care, but they don't pack away as small as down bags. Synthetic sleeping bags do retain most of their insulating properties, even if they become wet and are an incredibly durable and effective alternative.

Sleeping bags come in all shapes and sizes and for good reason. The less empty space there is in your sleeping bag the more effective it will be at retaining heat. However, there is a fine balance between having enough space for comfort and being warm enough for a good night's sleep.

A tapered bag follows the contours of the body, will pack smaller than a non tapered bag and have good warmth to weight ratios. Draw cords at the shoulders and around the hood of the sleeping bag help to cinch in the opening and vastly reduce heat loss.

Stash pockets feature on some bags which are ideal for storing valuables and keeping them secure while you sleep.

One tip; left handed people often prefer a right handed zip and right handed people often find a left hand zip easier.

Pillow pockets and integrated pillows are often featured on less technical bags where weight isn't too much of an issue.

These come in handy for keeping your pillow in the right place, if you don't have a pillow they'll keep a few folded up layers in place under your head.

🚲 🚲 🚲

I've never used one but a sleeping bag liner will add warmth and protect the lining from body oils and dirt, prolonging the life of your sleeping bag. It's easier to clean a liner than a whole sleeping bag. They are available in fleece, cotton and silk and offer variable degrees of warmth and comfort as well as considerably different pack sizes.

🚲 🚲 🚲

Other essentials (in my mind) items include pegs and washing line. If camping, string up a short line and peg that day's rinsed cycling kit to dry. I took mine from an old rotary drier I was disposing of.

Even if you're not planning to cook, take cutlery / spork and a plate / bowl as they're indispensable for lunchtime picnics. Take metal in preference to plastic and make sure it's hardwearing and lightweight. A steel camping mug for that

🚲

"glass" of wine is useful; pretty much everything you can eat from a plate can be eaten from a shallow bowl.

Nice to have (will you be cooking each night?):

- Pillow
- Gas stove and cylinder
- Matches / lighter.
- A cloth and small bottle of detergent.
- Iodine / other water purification substances (if wild camping)

Some consider a pillow a luxury, but for many it's got to be worth a few extra grams. If you like a firmer pillow you should probably find a blow up design. Compressible pillows that squish down into a stuff sack will do just that as soon as you put your head on it and thus are more suited to those who like a soft pillow. If you want to shave the grams off your trip but don't want to sacrifice your pillow simply fold up a couple of dry layers and use those to rest your head. I have taken inflatable pillows on trips and I have used a folded fleece as a pillow, I'm still deciding which is best!

When touring, we often camp but don't take cooking gear (we do take eating gear!) as it's more stuff to lug about and if camping, which can be cheap then it's acceptable to offset the savings vs eating out (isn't it?). Many times, we've used a disposable BBQ to cook on the campsite - always good.

If you intend to cook while away, go for a small, light stove. Remember you can't take gas cylinders on planes. If flying, your stove will need to be compatible with brands of cylinder available at your destination.

Briefly, other options of items to take might include;

- Tea towel
- Can opener
- Chopping knife with sleeve (one with a sleeve so you don't slice your bag apart!)
- Herbs, spices light and can add variety to your meal
- Tea & coffee
- Camping cooking pots or mess tins; lightweight which won't ruin quickly from the stove
- Chopping board; lightweight plastic ones slide easily into the back of a pannier
- Wooden spoon
- Lighter

🚲 🚲 🚲

Electronics; My essential items:

- Mobile phone
- Camera
- Powerbank
- Chargers

🚲

All fairly obvious I would have thought. A Powerbank is a must if camping. Some recommend solar chargers, these are fine but the rate of charge is slow and they're really only effective in very strong, continual sunlight but they could be a lifesaver if you're really stuck.

Make sure you take a solution for backing up photos; this could be uploading to The Cloud for instance. Remember to stop for as many photo opportunities as possible. Some of the best views might not be straight ahead, stop and have a look around, back, front and up every once in a while.

Ensure your electronics are stored in a secure place, electronics cost a lot of money so make sure there's a nice, cushioned and waterproof section of your panniers for them.

Don't flash expensive gear around; no matter where you are, carrying lots of electronics gear could make you a target.

Voltage and plug types differ around the world, research your destination to see what kind of adaptors and / or converters you will need if you're taking any electronics.

Nice to have:

- Travel tripod
- Laptop and case

- Spare memory cards
- External Harddrive
- Speakers
- Headphones
- Spare batteries
- Wind up torch

🚲 🚲 🚲

Toiletries, Health & Medical; My essential items:

- Basic first aid kit including plasters, antiseptic, painkillers, antihistamine, bandages and any other medicines
- Sunscreen / insect repellent
- Small (travel) towel / microfibre
- Personal toiletries & shaving gear
- Toilet roll
- Hand sanitiser
- Wet / baby wipes

Make sure you know how to use or administer anything in your first aid kit.

Microfibre towel; these can be tiny and lightweight but in cold conditions they often don't wick enough water or dry efficiently. These are a good compromise; still lightweight and small but able to dry a lot of water and do dry quickly.

Personal toiletries are up to the individual, I use small bottles and bars of soap which I've liberated from hotel stays in the

🚲

past. I usually take an electric razor; it lasts for over a week on one full charge.

A toilet roll can be a godsend if you're caught short in the countryside and some campsites, especially in France don't provide toilet paper.

I took insect repellent to the Outer Hebrides, a known haunt of many biting bugs. The weather was breezy and showery most of the time so the bugs stayed away luckily but it's worth being prepared.

Nice to have:

- Tweezers
- Rehydration salts
- Sudocrem
- Foil Blanket

Sudocrem can be invaluable for any chafing.

Foil blankets take up no room but can provide a surprising amount of warmth if you get into difficult situations.

🚲 🚲 🚲

Other items – everything else; my essential items:

- Penknife / Swiss army knife / Leatherman
- Credit and debit cards

🚲

- Passport / visa
- Driving licence
- Glasses
- Foreign currency
- Health insurance card
- Travel insurance details
- Tickets / boarding cards
- Sewing kit
- Notebook
- Pen
- Dirty laundry bags
- Binoculars
- Snacks; nuts, energy bars
- Paper maps & guidebooks etc
- Book(s) i.e. novels
- Map(s)
- Guides to the region
- Pen
- Notebook

I've heard VISA debit cards are accepted in more cash machines around the world than any other but I've no personal evidence of this.

A Swiss army knife or similar is one of those items of bike touring gear that simply makes life a little easier on the road. Whether you use the corkscrew, bottle opener, or can opener the most, it's a collection of knives and tools in a compact unit.

⚝

Top of your kit bag has to be food because there's nothing worse than running out of fuel and becoming unable to cycle. Cereal bars or nuts etc are a must. On one occasion we cycled into a campsite in France on a Monday when nothing was open, a supply of snacks got us through an otherwise food free evening.

A cycle tour is a holiday so make sure you have good travel insurance purchased before departure.

Nice to have:

- Blanket / plastic sheet to sit on
- Lighter
- Whistle
- Compass
- Map holder
- Reading books
- Compass
- Money belt
- Rail card
- Small games or playing cards
- Ear plugs
- Shopping bag for that picnic

General tips and hints.

After a trip I always make a list of what I took and if it was good choice or not and refine my list. Did I not use something, did something break and did I have to buy something on route?

Never rely on electronics alone if you are on a bike tour into the unknown. Have a backup of cash and maps if you're not sure if you'll have access to electricity. Technology fails, a map won't!

A little trip bag is perfect to sit on the top tube and give you easy access to anything you don't want in your rear pockets.

If you're caught in the rain, put your foot in a plastic bag before putting on your over trousers, it can make it easier to avoid snags from wet shoes as you put your trousers on.

Plastic gloves from petrol stations are great to slip over your normal gloves in the rain.

Pack your kit in lots of small bags and write on them what's inside. Makes packing and unpacking much quicker and also provides some protection against rain.

If in doubt as to whether to pack something that you don't think is essential, consider whether or not you'll be able to buy it on route. If you're not sure and it's available on route, leave it behind.

Make a check list of the things you absolutely cannot do without and double check it every day before you leave (wallet, phone, passport, camera etc).

Cheap earplugs hardly add any weight, but are great for getting sleep on a busy campsite.

🚲 🚲 🚲

A blast from the past.

I checked my packing list and thought I'd double check the internet for anything I may have missed which others might find useful (I hadn't, luckily!). Whilst doing so, I came across a list from 1897 (scottstoll.com/a-bicycle-touring-packing-list-from-1897/) showing how times have very much changed.

I'm not going to reproduce all of it here but have pulled out a few highlights.

🚲

Essential items (a selection):

- Flannel shirt
- Flannel collar
- Necktie
- Pair stockings
- 1 flannel nightshirt
- Loofah
- Waterproof cape
- Fullers earth
- Cardigan
- Pugaree **
- Pocket lens
- Prayer book
- Sperm oil
- Barometer
- Pipe and tobacco
- White collars and cuffs
- Visiting cards
- Braces
- Small silk flag

** An Indian word for turban, or a scarf, usually pleated, around the crown of some hats, especially sun helmets.

Nice to have (a selection):

- Slippers
- Supply of tea
- Spare white collars
- Spare neckties
- Writing case

★

Note:

If travelling abroad take your money in the form of gold coins. A revolver is not considered necessary in the more civilised areas of Europe, but if accosted by footpads or brigands, inform them that you are British and display your Union flag.

Those were the days, a loofah and a barometer!

How do I carry my stuff?

Cidre with Altura panniers on the beach en route to Le Havre (2011).

So, your gear is now spread out on the bed in the spare room, how on earth should it be carried? Maybe panniers, frame bags / bikepacking bags, trailer or a combination? A word of warning though, the gear taken will inevitably expand to fill the space available!

Whatever your solution, a couple of fully laden practice cycles around the block is always encouraged.

If flying, remember to put liquids and sharp items in the hold of the plane and split gear between bags so all your socks aren't in one place in case a bag is lost on the flight.

Don't be tempted to carry anything on your back, touring with a rucksack is not the best idea, placing the weight on your bike can certainly save your shoulders and back from undue stress – and you won't get the sweaty back triangle!

🚲 🚲 🚲

Panniers.

Panniers can be bought at any good bike shop or online with The Pannier Shop (pannier.cc/products/shop) a good place to start; they also offer kit for hire   (pannier.cc/products/hire).

Once a daily routine develops, it becomes second nature knowing which pannier to open when certain gear is needed. This is certainly better than opening the large bag in a trailer, where everything can become mixed up becoming a real pain finding things.

Rear panniers are the storage option which most cyclists turn to when starting touring. For trips lasting just a few days and which do not require lots of gear, clothing and food, two rear

🚲

(or maybe front?) panniers may be all you need to carry your things. If you can't quite fit everything into two rear panniers, you can strap items onto your rack (most riders strap their tent to the top of the rear rack) and / or add other small bags, like a handlebar bag, top-tube bag or saddlebag. On longer journeys, you can add a front rack and a pair of front panniers to hold more gear.

Panniers offer roomy storage and are designed to clip onto the sides of front or rear racks and can be quickly removed so you can take the bags with you when you reach your destination. It's often possible to lift the entire bike complete with panniers, this is a lot quicker than unhooking a trailer and lifting both trailer and bike separately.

Many panniers are waterproof, so you don't have to worry about your things getting wet during a rainy ride; for those that aren't, consider packing your things in waterproof stuff sacks or using raincovers designed to go over your panniers.

🚲 🚲 🚲

Waterproof roll-top panniers are preferable and panniers are sold in different sizes, measured in litres with smaller ones

🚲

designed for the front of the bike. Rear panniers typically hold 25-70 litres and front panniers 15-30 litres.

As you might expect there are pros and cons of every touring set up. As far as panniers are concerned they can carry a larger volume of gear, are easy to pack, are easy and quick to take off and put on the bike. They do have a couple of disadvantages however, they are wider, potentially making navigating narrow trails difficult, they can't be mounted to every bike and a bike with panniers doesn't handle as well as one without.

The best cycling panniers will likely come with feet or stands on the bottom which stops them becoming worn after scraping on the ground and keeps them waterproof. Another difference you may want to think about is pockets. Some panniers have completely smooth sides while others have compartments on the sides where you can organize items you want to reach quickly.

When buying panniers, ask these questions:

- Are they waterproof (preferably without a rain cover)?
- Are they easy to quickly fix on and take off the bike?

128

- Do they have a shoulder strap and / or carry handle (makes easier to carry)?
- Do they have zips which tend to break after a lot of use?
- Do they have a reasonably stiff back where the pannier lays against the rack (some have a handy document wallet inside the stiff back)?
- Are they hard-wearing?
- Are they value for money (top of the range are not cheap)?
- Do they have a proven track record?
- Are they of correct size (volume in litres or dimensions in cm)?

For touring, I use a pair of Altura 56 litre Dryline rear panniers which have served me well for many years. I've had to re-fix the feet a couple of times and replace the nylon drawstring (a local boat chandler helped me with this).

⚲ ⚲ ⚲

Racks.

Pannier racks bolt directly to the frame (rear) or fork (front). Panniers secure to the racks with a plastic or metal hook system which varies by brand.

Racks are metal and because the rack attaches to the bike with screws, your bike will need compatible screw holes. All touring bikes will have these holes. There are other options; racks can be attached to the seat tube which is only suitable for lighter loads. Tailfin (tailfin.cc) in Bristol produce a range of carbon fibre racks for road bikes and gravel bikes which attach to the seat tube.

Touring bikes are usually fitted with rear pannier racks. If you're buying a new pannier rack go for a wide one. This way you can easily have your camping tent or sleeping gear strapped along it with panniers on either side. If it's too narrow it can be tricky loading things on and off. A bungee over the rack is a way of securing washing to dry or a waterproof top so it can be grabbed quickly.

🚲 🚲 🚲

How to Pack Panniers.

When doing a self-supported tour, you may need two (front or rear) or four panniers (two front and two rear) to fit all your gear, clothing and food. Even on a supported tour you may wish to pack your day stuff in one or a pair of small panniers.

When riding with panniers try and have the load on your bike evenly distributed front-to-back and side-to-side. This will

🚲

create a more stable ride, to achieve this, set your sleeping bag and tent aside and then pack approximately 60% of the weight in your two front panniers and 40% of the weight in your two rear panniers. Replace the same stuff into the same bag in the same order to maintain this balance.

If you're only taking enough stuff for one pair of panniers, many tourists will cycle with just front, personally I take just a rear pair. In spite of having all the weight on the back of the bike, it's not a huge issue when standing up going uphill.

When you strap the tent and sleeping bag onto your rear rack, as many riders do, you will have an evenly distributed load. You could use luggage scales to make sure you have the right distribution, but going by feel usually gets you close enough. My sleeping bag is small enough to go in a pannier so I only strap my tent to the rack.

Put everything back in the same place, if you don't find something where you first looked, when you find it; put it where you first looked because that's where you thought it was! Organisation is key to keeping track of your stuff.

🚲 🚲 🚲

🚲

What to Pack in Rear Panniers.

Use rear panniers for seldom-used gear: Rear panniers aren't easy to get into unless you get completely off your bike, so it's best to use them to hold items you don't need frequent access to. Things like your extra clothing, backpacking stove, cooking gear and extra food are good options.

If you're only using rear panniers and thus will be putting items in that you'll surely need during your ride, then keep those items near the top.

Put heavy items in low down to help keep your bike's center of gravity low helping maintain good stability while riding.

What to Pack in Front Panniers.

Use front panniers for frequently used items; front panniers are easier to get into than rear panniers. Often, all you must do is stop riding and reach over your handlebars to access a front pannier (whereas with a rear pannier, you'll have to dismount). This makes front panniers a great place for things like snacks and food for the day, a first-aid kid, bike tools and any clothing you want quick access to, such as raingear.

Again, put heavy items in low down to keep your bike's centre of gravity low but also try to keep items you're likely to need during the day from getting buried too deep.

Rack trunks sit on top of your rear rack. They are smaller than panniers but larger than saddlebags, making them a good in-between option for carrying clothes, food and other items you want to keep accessible. Rack trunks are more commonly used on day trips rather than multiday tours. Not a solution if you have your tent strapped on the rack of course but they can be used in addition to panniers.

Frame bags or Bikepacking Bags.

While racks and panniers are generally preferred by bicycle tourists who need to carry all of the necessities for weeks, months, or even years on the road, Bikepacking bags are often preferred by those who spend more time riding off-road, on long stretches of gravel roads and single track through rural or wilderness regions. Most bikepackers take a minimalist approach to packing to keep the bike lightweight and agile.

🚲

Bikepacking bags (or frame bags) are soft bags which attach directly to the frame of the bike with straps and / or Velcro, metal racks are not required.

Bikepacking Bags pros and cons.

Bikepacking bags are lighter than panniers because no heavy steel or aluminum racks are required to mount the bags and the bike handles better with bikepacking bags as the weight of your gear is close to the bike's centre of gravity.

Bikepacking bags can be mounted to any bike, useful if your bike doesn't have braze-ons for racks. This is particularly common on bikes with carbon fibre frames, full-suspension mountain bikes and folding bikes.

However, they offer less volume than panniers and are harder to pack as they are odd shapes, handlebar bags and seat bags are cylinders and frame bags are triangles for instance.

There is no right or wrong way to go about packing your gear on your bike with everyone developing a different system over time, usually through trial and error. You don't have to choose between bikepacking bags or panniers as you can mix and match your luggage.

134

⚴

🚲 🚲 🚲

Handlebar packs attach to the front of the handlebar, giving you a convenient place to keep things like snacks, sunglasses, phone, wallet and a spare tube. Some handlebar bags have a waterproof folder on top for displaying a map. Aim to put only about 2kg max of gear in here. More weight could be too much for the handlebar bag to support and it will raise the centre of gravity of your bike, resulting in a wobbly ride.

Saddle bags / seat bags / underseat bags are small bags which attach to the underside of the saddle, often used to stow bike tools and a spare tube.

Top-tube bags / bento bags attach to the top tube, behind the head tube. They are easy to get into while riding, making them a good spot to keep snacks, sunscreen and a phone.

🚲 🚲 🚲

Waterproof phone mounts are common; handy for photos or navigation. If used, many tourists have a phone mount on the handlebars but there are pouches which clip to the top tube. Additionally, waterproof map holders (for those of us who prefer a more traditional paper based approach!) can be

🚲

clipped to the handle bars. If you're following a way marked route it's unlikely you'll need to continually refer to a map.

Carrying water.

Most touring bike frames are fitted with two sets of braze-ons on the seat tube and / or down tube for two bottle cages; if not you can buy strap-on ones. Make sure the cages have a bit of give so you can adjust them for different sized bottles.

If you're cycling in hot weather don't underestimate how much water you'll need. This is especially important if you're going through remote regions. Make sure you have enough bottle cages or other places you can carry extra water.

I usually tour with two bottles, a godsend in hot weather, hydration is crucial when cycling for any period of time especially the hot tour of 2019. I usually take two 750ml Bidons. If it's very hot, you'll need a lot of water so consider dissolving a High 5 Zero electrolyte tablet or similar in one of the 750ml Bidons, tastes a bit funny but helps to replace some sweated out salts.

Another option is a backpack with a water bladder (I've never used one) but it can make sipping on the go very easy. It's really no problem stopping for a drink, it's a skill but it's also fairly easy to grab your Bidon and drink while cycling. Water has got to be your number one essential, you can't assume shops will be open, or indeed that you'll be anywhere near one when you need that thirst-quenching glug. Whenever you get the chance to top up those Bidons, do.

🚲 🚲 🚲

Dry bags.

A must for any cycling trip, even if your panniers are waterproof it's good to get a few just to be on the safe side. They're cheap, lightweight and come in a variety of sizes. Use them for electronics and valuables; keeping all of your clothes in one also means it's quick and easy to take them out and store. If all else fails, a strong plastic bag will suffice. They're also good for keeping dirty and clean kit apart.

Handlebar mirror(s).

Some tourists swear by a mirror. It's useful for checking if your buddies are still behind but is absolutely no substitute for looking behind. I don't use them.

🚲 🚲 🚲

🚲

Bell and lights.

You're now in danger of having an overcrowded handlebar! A bell is essential to warn others of your approach. Please check local laws but in the UK new bikes must be sold with one but you don't have to have one on your bike. This means you could remove it immediately after purchase.

I've already recommended taking lights but ensure there's room on the bar!

Rucksack.

I'm not recommending cycling with one but take a small one as a light day pack as you're not going to spend the whole time on your bike. Even if you're going have your head down for most of the trip, it's also useful when buying food or supplies.

🚲 🚲 🚲

Trailers.

Whether you use a trailer is a personal choice but some tourists combine panniers and trailers. Other tourers will use a trailer instead of some or all of their panniers because they have bulky gear which fits better in a trailer and / or they

🚲

prefer the way the bike handles. The right combination of trailer and panniers depends on personal preference and how much stuff you have.

For many self-supported riders on a long journey, a cargo trailer and two rear or front panniers will provide ample room for packing. Remember, you may need to be able to lift your bike over a wall, up stairs; etc a trailer may make these tasks more complicated. Andrew P Sykes managed to complete three long tours only using only 4 panniers, it can be done!

Bicycle trailers come in various guises and designs, although the general theory is the same in that the bulk of a load is towed behind the bicycle. The trailer itself will be designed to contain a large bag, or panniers on either side of an "extra-wheel".

One of the benefits of using a trailer over panniers, is it puts a lot less stress on the bicycle's rear wheel, reducing the risk of broken spokes and possible damage to the rear hub. This is due to the way in which the weight is distributed.

A downside to this is there are one or more extra wheels on the trailer so the chances of punctures increase and spare tubes specific to the trailer may need to be carried.

Another good thing about using a bicycle trailer over panniers is the entire "train" is more aerodynamic than when using panniers.

Any gain is offset by the overall set-up being heavier, the main plus on the side of using a trailer, is that it enables you to carry more stuff when needed.

How do I pack my stuff?

A transporter bridge across the Charente River, France. That was fun! (2015).

As mentioned above, remember weight distribution between front and rear panniers and ensuring your load is balanced.

Many bike tourers can fit everything they need for a ride in front and / or rear panniers and strapped to their racks. Keep in mind, though, with each bag you add, you increase the weight you must pedal uphill. So, really do think about whether extra bags and / or stuff are necessary or if the items you would put in them can fit just as well in your panniers.

Sort out your options in good time.

Spend some time going through different pannier and packing options to see what works well for you. This also means thinking about how you arrange the items inside the panniers. At the end of a hard day, you want to know where everything is and be able to access it quickly rather than emptying your life on the side of the road every evening.

Make sure you have extra room.

If your panniers are completely full you won't have any room for extra food, supplies or water. Cramming fit to bursting will cause problems unpacking and finding stuff easily.

Go on a test run.

No matter how good it looks, or however many times you've practised loading up your bike, go on a fully-loaded test run as the time to test all your shiny, new gear is not on day one of your trip! Decide what does and doesn't work, refine and try again.

A bike loaded with gear will feel different than one that's not; with a little practice you'll be able to pack your things so they remain accessible during the ride without greatly impacting

142

🚲

the stability and performance of your bike. A bicycle weighed down with stuffed panniers feels and handles a differently than a lightweight road bike. It might change your mind as to how much stuff to take as well!

One of the specific areas to test is riding downhill as loaded bikes can get bad "shimmies" when going downhill.

🚲 🚲 🚲

How to pack.

Roll clothing up and remember to leave a bit of space for daily purchases and other items you might pick up along the way. You'll want to keep things like your wallet, camera, maps and tools easily accessible, maybe utilising a handlebar or saddle pack. Try and keep your total luggage load beneath 20kg.

You won't need as much as you think you do. Beginners typically bring more gear, food and clothing than they need (I'm still guilty of this!), which adds weight taking up precious space in panniers.

Don't carry more than about one day's worth of food unless you're biking in remote areas without access to shops, markets

143

🚲

or restaurants. It's often helpful to use a checklist so you won't forget items or bring too much. When considering the weight of how much you're carrying, it's worth checking for load limits for both your bike and front and rear racks.

🚲 🚲 🚲

Bring no more than three or four days' worth of clothes; it's easy to pack more clothing than you really need. For any trip lasting more than a few days (including those that last weeks or even months), don't bring more than about three or four days' worth of clothes (shorter trips generally require less). You can wash your clothes along the way, either at a Launderette or in sinks with some travel soap, strapping items to your rear rack to dry while you ride. You will be in biking clothes far more often than non biking clothes, so select items which you're comfortable riding in but will also work if you take a day off. For instance, rather than wearing cycling jerseys and tight, stretchy shorts, many bike tourers opt for synthetic shirts with a casual style and baggy mountain bike shorts because they work well for biking and walking through town.

🚲 🚲 🚲

🚲

Pack only the essential repair items; consider their benefit to you while thinking about how close your route is to civilisation, your mechanical skills and the amount of weight the parts add to your load.

🚲 🚲 🚲

When you're getting ready for your trip, lay everything out on the floor or a bed so you can see exactly what you're taking. This will help you remember to bring what you need and keep you from packing things you don't. You can then use small stuff sacks or zip-top plastic bags to organise your possessions. This works especially well for clothing; pack one outfit per stuff sack or plastic bag and when you're ready for a wardrobe change on your trip, all you have to do is grab a stuff sack or bag rather than digging around for individual items.

Put everything back in its place, where is your rain jacket when it starts to pour? If you decide to keep your rain jacket near the top of your front left pannier, put it there every time.

Keep important items within easy reach. Things like your phone, wallet, passport, tools etc should always be kept in a spot that you can easily access.

🚲

Learn as you go. There's no one right way to pack for bike touring, so with each bike trip keep a list and refine during and after each trip. What worked and what didn't? Make a list and then check it off.

Have lists for different scenarios i.e. hiring bike and camping; taking own bike and not camping; hot weather, cool weather etc.

Learn how to make the most of limited packing space: Stuff hollow items (like shoes, helmets and water bottles) with other small items (socks, etc.). Roll clothes to eliminate air and reduce wrinkles.

On most bicycle tours, you're on the move with little time for laundry and drying. When possible, travel with fast-drying clothing. Synthetic fabrics are not only the most breathable and quick drying, they can also be the easiest to pack (the worst fabric to ride in is cotton).

How do I plan my trip?

The Loire Valley route markers – very easy to follow (2012).

The route and the ultimate destination is the most important element of your cycling trip both in terms of daily destination but also how far you plan to travel each day and the pace. Don't try and cram too much into a day, you need time for sight-seeing.

For many the idea of a cycling tour is to just get on the bike and hit the open road and see where you end up. While that sounds a wonderful way to spend your time, it's wise to be sure there are accommodation options available to you each evening. Booking before you travel (if a short tour) or a few days in advance (if a longer tour) will ensure you have a place to stay. Booking in advance can also save money by taking advantage of special deals.

My early trips and the first couple I completed with my usual group involved minimal planning. We knew where we were going and had booked essentials such as cross channel ferries but apart from that, we had no plan. This is fine if you're confident of getting to your destination in time for the ferry home or if you're not unduly bothered about knowing if you'll have somewhere to stay each night. When things haven't gone as well as might be expected, something usually comes up. For instance, I've slept on a windowsill of a casino near Avranches in France (I was 17) and on another occasion we arrived at a campsite which was full but we were allowed to pitch our small tents on the grassy roundabout at the entrance to the site (for a very reduced fee!).

Planning some or all of your trip is a good idea if you're on a tight timescale or have a deadline, a plane or train to catch or have to go back to work on a certain day. Planning can throw up issues with the proposed route; do you plan to finish a day's ride in the middle of nowhere for instance? Can you avoid that steep hill by sneaking around the bottom on a farm track?

Planning using maps can also show interesting places to visit or a potential diversion and it gives peace of mind and a calmer experience but don't be afraid to tweak the route before or during your trip.

Planning was key to my successful solo trip to the Outer Hebrides. I had to get to the start and home from the finish, no mean feat. Also, places to stay on the islands were few and far between so I booked everything before I left home to ensure I had a bed for the night.

🚲 🚲 🚲

On both of my solo trips, I created a set of daily cue sheets. These are notes on the day's cycling showing major places, mileages, anything which I might want to / need to detour to see and anything on the route to watch out for (hills, bad signage). I also added details of the night's accommodation i.e. contact details, name, address and a small map if necessary so I didn't have to faff about on arrival trying to find the place. The Outer Hebrides trip was fine in that it was

🚲

easy to follow the route and I was on a series of islands so it wasn't difficult to get lost. I had maps as well, a couple of times on the C&C route I did take a wrong turn so used the paper maps and Google maps to get me back on track. I printed them and had a sheet per day, stored in plastic wallets in my pocket, they were invaluable. I could also make notes on them to help me in writing up the trip afterwards.

The time of year can dictate how much you might want to plan. For instance, the south of France can be very busy in summer so places to stay; including campsites may be fully booked.

Consider how long you should ride for; both in terms of days, but also hours per day. Cycling in very hot weather can be difficult for obvious reasons; the heat can be very demanding of your body, testing your stamina.

Cycling through heavy rain or wind etc. is equally challenging and demanding. Make sure you consider this and check weather forecasts before you arrange your trip. It will also impact the equipment you'll need to take with you.

Break up the day into manageable chunks, use refreshment breaks or tourist attractions along the way as designated rest stops. Give yourself enough time; allow yourself most of the day, set off reasonably early and take the best part of the day to cycle. There shouldn't be any need to hurry unduly.

It is generally cooler and less windy first thing in the morning and starting early means if you want to have a long lunch or visit somewhere, you won't be cycling late into the evening looking for a place to stay – you have time.

Make the most out of every opportunity. If you find a source of water, fill up all your bottles. If you find a small shop in the middle of nowhere, buy food, as it may be the last shop for a while. If you're in a bar or restaurant, sit near a socket and (asking permission first) charge up your electronic gear. Some places will happily charge your gear behind the bar. They will be more inclined to help if you're buying food and / or drink of course.

It's important to make some sort of itinerary of your schedule before you set off even if it's as high level as "arrive in xyz before 17:00" and try to stick to it as much as possible. This will give you an idea of how much distance you need to be travelling per day in order to stay on course allowing you to make the necessary travel and accommodation arrangements in advance.

🚲 🚲 🚲

How many of you are travelling? This will have an impact on the best time for you to travel as members of your party might only be able to travel a certain stretch of the route before needing to go back to work, for example. This happened on the Loire trip, one of our group had just started a new contract so had to leave us after a week. We had to be in a town or city which had a railway station so Orleans was our destination. We did have a contingency plan as the Loire shares its valley with a railway for most of its route so we had plenty of options in the end. Similarly, on the Black Forest trip, one of us couldn't travel out with the group so we arranged to be in Basle on a certain day to meet him.

If you're planning to ride solo you may feel you'd prefer to plan more rigorously as there isn't the group dynamic involved in agreeing where to go and by when, it's all up to you so why not set it in stone before you leave and be done with it?

152

🚲

For longer tours try and build in a luxury day every so often. Maybe a night in a decent hotel or a day off the bike and two nights in the same place? On a trip of a week or more, we usually stay two nights in the same place (usually camping) and have a day off the bike or cycle with minimal baggage to explore the local area.

Have at least one day when you haven't planned anything at all. Just amble along until you get somewhere interesting, then stay there.

It's not always about the distance, there will be places and things you just want to stop and see. The idea of travelling is to experience places and things and to meet people.

🚲 🚲 🚲

Planning can go wrong, on two trips, one along the Canal du Midi and the other along the Loire Valley we took lists of campsites on our route but came unstuck a couple of times. On the Canal du Midi trip, the site had closed for the winter (it was early September!) and during the Loire trip, the site in Orleans had closed some years before. On both occasions, it was late afternoon and the next campsite was a few km along the road so we decided to stay put. We were told by a

🚲

passerby on the Canal du Midi trip to wild camp by the side of sports pitches on the banks of the canal and in Orleans we found a cheap hotel.

The wild camping worked well until we awoke to the sound of grunting outside. Peeking out we saw soldiers of the French Foreign Legion (FFL / *Légion étrangère*) doing physical education. Big blokes all, we were slightly concerned but they continued their exercises while we struck camp and cycled swiftly away.

It's possible to over plan (I've never been guilty of this!) so I like to strike a balance of booking the essentials such as transport, maybe the first and last night's accommodation and try and be in an area each night which will have accommodation and / or shops for food. If everything is planned to the smallest detail, it's necessary to stick to the schedule removing any scope for a detour or stopping in a different place.

Planning too much can be counterproductive on long-term tours (more than one month) but it can be very important when your time is limited. If you have a return train on a certain date and time, you have to be there.

🚲

Strike a happy medium, it can be difficult in a group (you can spilt the planning between you of course) as some will want to plan more than others, you will have differing strengths and interests so use them. Going solo, what you do is completely up to you. Not having anywhere to stay can mean a certain amount of faffing about looking for somewhere or going to tourist information centres etc which, after a few hours in the saddle is not as much fun as finding a bar and a beer.

🚲 🚲 🚲

Know your limits; don't plan to cycle too far each day. If there are major climbs involved or somewhere you want to visit then reduce even more. This figure will change depending on the rider, you may be a well trained weekend cyclist but cycling with a load is totally different. My longest day on my most recent trip (on the flat) was 80km (as I had stopped slightly short of where I thought I would the previous night) but another day was 40km as I wanted to visit a couple of places and there was a hill on part of the route.

Think about the route, the main road might be the most direct route but try and stick to secondary roads or

🚲

designated cycle paths. It's no fun cycling on busy roads just because it's the shortest way. Cycle touring is not about the destination, it is about riding in beautiful locations, a long stretch alongside the A1 might get you there sooner but it won't be beautiful. The UK Sustrans routes are on minor roads or paths but are rarely the most direct route to places.

🚲 🚲 🚲

I'm a paper map fan, you can't beat them as far as I'm concerned, I find it easier to visualise the route and see what's in areas away from the planned route which I may wish to visit. There are plenty of apps to assist with which I'm not very familiar but I have recently started recording my rides on Strava.

I have used Cycle Streets as an aid before trips and Google Maps on my phone while on route, usually when I'm a bit lost!

An internet search will throw up many apps including Komoot, OsmAnd, Galileo, RideWithGPS.com, OpenStreetMap, Mapmyride and Cycle.Travel. I have no experience of these so I suggest do plenty of research, ask around then pick your favourite.

🚲

Paper or electronic maps are indispensable aids for both planning and executing tours. Apart from possible tearing, paper maps won't fail you. Well, they did once (or maybe it was "user error"); on a trip in western France, we checked the maps over breakfast, decided which camp site to aim for and set off. The trouble was, we moved from one map to another and didn't line them up properly. French road numbering can seem quite random at times so we decided it was the fault of the French. After cycling for ages and passing the same house three times, we had another, closer look and realised we hadn't joined them at the correct place and were only 10km from the campsite!

For both practical and safety reasons, you should have a good awareness of what lays off and around the designated route (doubly true when touring in remote areas), which is difficult to get in an app. You might spot something which would be good to visit on a detour or a picnic spot which you might not have seen on an app. Bigger maps, not surprisingly, give a better idea of the bigger picture than do the GPS maps on handhelds and other electronic devices.

There's nothing better for show-and-tell when you return home than a big fold-out map with your route highlighted.

止

That said, the technology available today for route planning and navigating is incredible and it will only improve with time.

Choose maps and apps wisely, some applications have maps only for certain continents while others might not include trails or paths.

🚲 🚲 🚲

I've touched on way marked trails such as Eurovelo, Voie Vert and Sustrans, all of which have excellent online mapping tools. They're designed for cyclists and walkers and are off the main roads so why not use them when possible?

Another advantage of a way marked route is the signage is usually excellent. Having said that, if you're following a river or canal route, it's fairly obvious if you've taken a wrong turn!

Sustrans use excellent blue signs denoting the NCN number (i.e. 780) and / or route name (i.e. Hebridean Way). They often include major place names and distances. Be aware some signs might be indicating large towns near the route. Thinking I had to go there, in 2020 I spent an extra hour

🚲

detouring in and out of Galasheils, not a huge issue in the end but I should have cycled around the edge!

Eurovelo use the EU flag with the route number in the centre to denote where you are. Named routes i.e. Black Forest and Loire use their own logos which are easy to spot. In many places, there are local signs to the next village; these are useful if you know whether or not the village is on the route.

One source of possible confusion are points at which various routes merge and / or cross leading to a proliferation of signs as routes become shared.

歲 歲 歲

In the UK, we're lucky to have the Ordnance Survey (ordnancesurvey.co.uk) which has been producing maps since 1791. They produce a range of excellent maps in paper (some in plastic, laminated versions – the "active" versions) and online forms. The versions most useful for cyclists are the "leisure series" and include the following:

Tour.

These are one sheet maps on a scale of 1:100,000 covering a generally county-sized area, showing major and most minor roads and containing tourist information and selected footpaths. Tour maps are generally produced from enlargements of 1:250,000 mapping. Several larger scale town maps are provided on each sheet for major settlement centres.

OS Landranger.

Using a scale of 1:50,000, they are the "general purpose" map covering the whole of Great Britain and the Isle of Man. The map shows all footpaths and the format is similar to the Explorer maps (see below), but with less detail. This is the most useful of the OS maps as it has a wealth of tourist information at a good scale showing all the major and minor roads, footpaths, byways and the National and Local cycle routes in good detail. Contours are marked at 10m vertical intervals, giving you a good idea of the ascents and descents in hilly terrain.

They have all the usual tourist information including Youth Hostels and most of the main campsites are marked. Usefully the legend is translated into French and German.

OS Explorer.

Using a scale of 1:25,000 they are specifically designed for walkers and cyclists and cover Great Britain (but not the Isle of Man). These are the most detailed leisure maps that Ordnance Survey publish and cover all types of footpaths and most details of the countryside for easy navigation. The OS-branded sheets within the Explorer series show areas of greater interest in England and Wales (such as the Lake District, the Black Mountains etc.) with an enlarged area coverage. In May 2015, Ordnance Survey announced that the new release of OL series maps would come with a mobile download version, available through a dedicated app on Android and iOS devices.

Marvelous Maps.

A newcomer to UK maps are the Marvelous Maps series (Marvellousmaps.com) a selection of themed maps around which it might be possible to build a tour.

Examples include the Place Names Map; rude-sounding place names. Maybe the Literature Map is for you; chapter and verse on literary Britain, with thrillingly plotted places of poetry, prose and page-turning trivia.

161

澶

Two others are the Food and Drink Map; full-to-bursting with over 2,000 food and drink locations and the Film and TV map; an ensemble cast of famous film and TV locations in the UK.

Goldeneye Guides to Cycling Country Lanes and Byways.

See goldeneyeguides.co.uk for details, these are a series of 15 laminated maps covering some of the most interesting cycling areas in England. They show the National and Local cycle way marked routes, also marked are circular family traffic-free cycling trails.

At this scale the maps are clear and there is enough detail for easy navigation. They contain tourist information including Youth Hostels and many campsites. Terrain is shown using a 50m shading system. There is a handy index to the towns and villages on the map and on the reverse are descriptions on most of the major places of interest.

In Europe, Michelin produce a huge range of maps and guides for not just Europe, many places in the world. Maps are 1:150,000, 1:200,000 or 1:4,000,000 scales or city plans at 1:12,500 or 1:15,000 scales. In France (and its overseas territories), the IGN (Institut Geographic National) maps are indispensible and are produced in a range of 1:25,000 to 1:100,000.

🚲 🚲 🚲

As well as a map (or maybe instead of as they usually contain excellent maps), consider a guide book.

The publishers Verlag Esterbauer produce a large range of "Bikeline" cycle-specific guides under a sub brand, Cycline. Covering many popular long distance routes they are mainly in German but some routes have been translated into English. I've used these (both in German and English) for trips along the Elbe, Weser and the Black Forest in Germany. We mainly used the excellent maps so the German text wasn't an issue. They also produce guides for routes in other countries i.e. the Loire Valley in France.

Bikeline books are excellent for planning before you go and for detailed, turn-by-turn route instructions during the trip. If you want a detailed map with short lists of B&Bs, hotels, camp sites, places to eat and bike repair shops, this is good stuff.

🚲

Cicerone (cicerone.co.uk) produce a large number of very comprehensive cycling and walking guides for the UK and many other countries, they were invaluable for my Loire and Outer Hebrides trips.

On a smaller scale, Offcomers (theoffcomers.co.uk) produce a select number of guides; I used the excellent Hebridean Way guide for my 2019 trip. The full list is The Caledonian Way (Sustrans route 78), one each for walking and cycling the Hebridean Way (Sustrans route 780), the V4 Brittany cycle Route and the Bay cycle Way. The maps are excellent and the text is clear and concise detailing the route, things to look out for and some possible detours you may wish to take. Highly recommended.

Cycling UK currently produce two guides, one for the recently opened 200 mile King Alfred's Way in southern England and the other for the 800 mile Great North Way from the Peak District to Cape Wrath and John o' Groats.

In recent years, Sustrans have been creating a number of named and themed routes from their numbered routes in the UK. For instance, the Coast and Castles (south) route which I completed in 2020 uses part of NCN 1 and the Hebridean Way is NCN 780.

For many of these, they produce guide books and / or waterproof maps; scale 1:100,000 which are excellent.

All the guides I have seen or used from Sustrans, Cicerone, Offcomers and Cycling UK have been written by cyclists who have completed each route so is written from a position of experience. Some have differing editions, try and use the most up to date.

🚲 🚲 🚲

There are an increasing number of popular way-marked cycling routes in the UK which might be a good choice for a first trip. Some of the most popular include (this is not a full list by any means):

Lands End to John O'Groats (LeJog).

This classic long-distance bike tour is a tough but incredible way to see Britain. You'll need at least 10 days minimum to do it, even by the most direct main roads, but longer is recommended. It's better to treat yourself to a few more days off and take the most scenic routes so could take up to two or three weeks but it'll be worth it. cycle-endtoend.org.uk.

Coast to Coast (C2C).

The 147 mile C2C Coast-to-Coast route across the north of England takes you through the stunning scenery of the northern Lakes, the Northern Pennines and then the Durham Dales before you dip your tyres in the North Sea. C2c-guide.co.uk.

Coast and Castles (south).

This 200 mile ride from Newcastle to Edinburgh passes ancient settlements, abbeys and castles as it passes through Northumberland and the Scottish Borders. Coast-and-castles.co.uk. There is a north section which runs from Edinburgh to Aberdeen.

Wales' Celtic Trail.

From Swansea to Fishguard, this is the hillier half of a route that links Chepstow on the Bristol Channel to Wales' west coast, 143 miles long with many family sections; this route has plenty of coastal gems and historic sites.

West Country Way.

This 252 mile route from Padstow to Bristol and Bath includes Bodmin Moor, Exmoor and will take you at least eight days to ride; possibly more. westcountryway.co.uk.

Reivers Cycle Route.

A 170 mile coast-to-coast cycle route from Tynemouth to Whitehaven through Northumberland and the Kielder Forest. The route takes in Carlisle and the Lake District and provides a great alternative or return route for C2C. reivers-guide.co.uk.

The Hebridean Way.

200 miles across 10 islands of the Outer Hebrides, stunning scenery at every turn. visitouterhebrides.co.uk/hebrideanway.

Lôn Las Cymru.

A 250 mile cycle from Holyhead to Cardiff or Chepstow, using minor roads, railway paths, forestry tracks and ancient coach roads. There are some tough challenges as the route crosses the Snowdonia National Park and the range of the Cambrian Mountains. cycle.travel/route/lon_las_cymru.

King Alfred's Way.

This is billed as a Bikepacking route as over half is off road on tracks and bridleways. It is a 200 mile circular route starting and finishing in Winchester where King Alfred is buried. The route runs around historic Wessex, the Anglo-Saxon kingdom of Alfred the Great and connects iconic monuments including Stonehenge, Avebury stone circle, Iron Age hill forts, Farnham Castle, and Winchester and Salisbury Cathedrals. cyclinguk.org/king-alfreds-way.

The Great North Trail.

Another bikepacking route running from the Peak District to Cape Wrath / John O'Groats taking the rider over rolling hills and dales to remote windswept moorland, crumbling castles to hidden waterfalls, swooping single-track and old Roman roads and everything in between. The nature of the route varies in different areas - from rugged upland trails across exposed moorland, suitable for more experienced mountain bikers, to sections of canal path and disused railway perfect for family days out. cyclinguk.org/offroadcampaigns/great-north-trail.

🚲 🚲 🚲

🚲

OK, you've decided where you'd like to go and assembled any maps and books, what next?

Whether using maps, apps, or a combination, try to find the elevation profile of the route you're considering. A lot of big climbs and descents make for more difficult, but sometimes more interesting, biking.

Keep in mind the distance between services and water refill opportunities.

Start preparing your trip a few weeks before and make lists with everything you need or have to organise. Make sure to adapt them to the peculiarities of your trip, the expected weather conditions and the destination or route you have chosen.

Remember that travelling isn't about covering as many miles as you can, set a destination according to your abilities, ride at your own pace and enjoy the experience.

Think about how many hours you are going to pedal each day and when you will do it. When it's summer and the sun is strong, it's best to leave early in the morning. Don't overdo it in the first couple of days.

169

Give yourself days to sit back and rest. This helps you recharge your batteries and gives you time to take in the sights and other cultural highlights of the trip. The challenge is to create an optimal balance between recreation and riding.

So that you don't have to struggle to find suitable accommodation at day's end, if you're not booking all accommodation, make sure you've booked a day or two in advance at a minimum.

Think about detours, side trips and anything you'd like to see on the way, a castle and a beach for instance.

Consider a plan B if the weather doesn't behave or if there's illness, injury or a serious bike issue, will you be near a railway station for instance so you can catch a train out of trouble?

Blogs and other online resources.

There are many online resources, too many to list here but some ofg my favouriets inlicde:

- cyclingeurope.org
- Bicycletouringpro.com

170

- tomsbiketrip.com
- freewheelingfrance.com
- biketouringtips.com

Also worth checking out is philosophyonabike.com but I'm biased as it's the son of a friend of mine – Marcus Macdonald writing about his adventures cycling around the world.

Where could I stay at night?

Hire bikes sheltering from the heat, near Montpellier. Yes, there was a bottle of wine cooling in the fountain! (2019).

The answer depends on a number of factors, time of year (is it likely to be cold and / or wet?), cost (how deep are your pockets?) and amount of gear you're prepared to carry about (which might rule out camping).

Probably the first decision is whether to camp or not. Are you a seasoned camper, do you have the gear and are you going to an area with plenty of campsites? Camping can be inexpensive and you're more independent and closer to nature.

On the other hand, staying in hotels means you may be more comfortable, your washing will dry; you are guaranteed to be able to charge your tech and will have less gear to carry.

It's fairly easy to book accommodation either from the UK or on arrival at your destination. Tourist Information offices, chambers of commerce, convention and visitor's associations and many internet resources list information about hotels, campsites, B&Bs and other lodgings. Many maps and guides, especially the Bikeline and Cicerone series list local options. The OS, Michelin, Sustrans and IGN maps show campsites so can be useful for planning.

🚲 🚲 🚲

It is possible to wild camp; this could be through choice or necessity. It can have its downsides, on the Outer Hebrides, I came across two French cyclists who had wild camped in a farmer's field during a storm and the farmer had taken pity and rescued them during the night. I found them sheltering sitting next a pile of wet stuff looking rather miserable so

🚲

spent half an hour or so helping them to make sense of the big pile of wet stuff.

Wild camping is legal in some countries – check for local rules. In the UK it's legal in Scotland (check outdooraccess-scotland.scot) but be considerate on where you choose to pitch your tent. If possible ask around, it was a local who suggested where we should camp by the Canal du Midi.

When you leave in the morning, leave nothing behind, this is true of any camp site of course.

🚲 🚲 🚲

If you're planning to visit an area rich in campsites; areas of France being an example, you will be spoilt for choice. Take a list of local campsites so you can set a target for the day's cycling and have enough information to be able change plans (i.e. go to another site) if your chosen site is full, closed or not accepting tents. The latter happened to us; in 2019 on a trip to the Montpellier area a couple of campsites had stopped taking tents as they had converted camping pitches to holiday cabins which was disappointing.

174

🚲

Many urban areas in France have municipal camp sites, free of frills but very cheap and usually in the centre of town, highly recommended.

There is no overall governing body for campsites in the UK and no national standards or recognised star rating for the facilities that are available at each site. The quality and amount of facilities can vary from site to site. Usually most sites will offer pitches for tourers on a per person basis which includes washrooms, showers and a washing up point. Some sites include free showers but some will be on a coin or token metered system. Usually in France, we pay for one pitch (un emplacement) with 5 tents taking up the same area as one family tent or van making it very affordable.

There are many websites listing UK campsites, here is a selection; campsites.co.uk, camp-sites.co.uk, coolcamping.com, pitchup.com – there are plenty more.

Local tourist information offices will help you; they've helped a great deal on our French and German trips but don't assume they're always open, the French ones tend to close for a long lunch but they are usually open until later in the evening.

🚲 🚲 🚲

Believe it or not, you don't have to be a youth to stay in a youth hostel! I've stayed in youth hostels in Bordeaux, Tours, Rennes and Basle. They are cheap and clean accommodation which it's possible to book from the UK prior to travel or just turn up as we did in Tours. In French; auberge de jeunesse and in German, Jugendherberge.

If one of the group joins the YHA prior to the trip, it's often possible to obtain a discount; well worth considering.

In the UK, the YHA (yha.org.uk) which has 200 hostels across England and Wales or Scottish YHA (hostellingscotland.org.uk) which has 70 hostels across Scotland are the places to go if a night in a hostel is your choice.

The days of having to do chores are long gone but you will have to make and strip your bed. Single or double rooms may be available along with the more traditional dormitories where you may have to share with strangers.

🚲 🚲 🚲

🚲

Hotels, guest houses and B&Bs can increase the cost of your trip but you will have to lug less stuff about and be able to sleep in a bed rather than on a mat. It's all a question of budget.

Chain hotels; Premier Inn and Travelodge in the UK, Formule 1 in France for instance provide no frills experiences and can throw up some very cheap deals especially if you book in advance. If you ask for a room on the ground floor, it's sometimes possible to wheel your bike into the room overnight.

Some hotels positively encourage cyclists to stay, especially if they're on a well ridden route. The Lindisfarne Inn in Beal is on the Coast and Castles (south) route and provides a huge lockable bike shed, tools, pump and bike washing facilities. This is in addition to excellent accommodation and it's a pub which serves good food, all good.

Always tell the accommodation you will be arriving by bike and ask if there's anywhere secure and dry the bike can be kept overnight, I've never been refused and my bike has rested in sheds, basements and in my room.

🚲 🚲 🚲

🚲

Consider hospitality networks such as Warmshowers (warmshowers.org) for cyclists and Couchsurfing (couchsurfing.com) for all travelers, not just cyclists. These sites offer alternatives to paid accommodation.

They are communities of people offering beds for travelers, usually in their homes, Warmshowers started in 2005 and now have over 100,000 members worldwide.

It's possible to receive home-cooked dinners, breakfasts and even packed lunches. Search for hosts who offer food— look for "Food: Yes" on the app.

It goes without saying, always offer to help cook and clean up. Say thanks and leave positive reviews.

Slightly more radical but a couple of friends of mine have recently stopped working and started house-sitting, using the house as a base for trips but this is a long term option and does tie you into one place.

How fit do I have to be?

Ferry 'cross the Weser (2018).

You don't have to be super fit to tour, there's no need to have thighs like Chris Hoy or stick thin legs like Chris Froome but you should have a decent base level of fitness however small that might be! This will mean you can go further and cope with hills or headwinds and generally enjoy yourself. It's supposed to be fun after all.

You will get noticeably fitter during a tour, it doesn't take long. If you're a regular cyclist, a commuter for instance, you

179

should be ok to handle a couple of hours in the saddle; if you can cycle a bike you can go touring.

Max Glaskin tells me that regular exercise can increase life expectancy by two years and a cyclist can have a physiology of a person 10 years younger than a non cyclist of the same age.

Cycling is good for the heart (which is a muscle after all) and can increase maximum oxygen uptake and the older you get, the better riding a bike is for you.

🚲 🚲 🚲

The British Cycling website is a must-visit containing loads of hints and tips about all things cycling. One article about cycling at different ages caught my eye. The key points are set out below.

Cycling is genuinely a sport for all ages and there's no reason why it can't be a lifelong pleasure. However, in order to get the most out of your cycling, it's essential to take your age into consideration.

In your 20's it's important to realise that you're not indestructible and important to remember that you might

🚲

still be growing well into your mid-twenties so check your set-up and position on the bike regularly, especially if you start developing any unusual aches or niggles. You'll also have a high metabolism so ensure you fuel well, get plenty of sleep and don't burn the candle at both ends too much. With a high proportion of lean body mass, excellent rebound strength from your tendons and high oxygen uptake rate, your strengths will be short, hard and explosive efforts. Weaknesses will include aerobic endurance and your riding economy.

The bad news is that when you reach your 30s, your body is starting to decline and losing some of its top end performance. Injuries will take a little longer to heal and muscle soreness will linger.

The decline in top end performance and other issues that you may have noticed in your 30s will accelerate into your 40s. Get small niggles looked at and sorted out and if you've lost some mobility, work on this and change your position on the bike if necessary.

Good nutrition is vital as it can help manage hormonal changes and there's no doubt, if you put on a few pounds, they'll be far harder to shift than 10-15 years ago!

🚲

Any losses you experienced in your 40s will be magnified in your 50s. However, if you only come to cycling in your 50s, you can still make progress.

Be aware of increased chances of injury. Keep moving, the body is meant to move. The more we move the more muscle we keep and the easier it is to do things. Resistance training should be a real priority, even if you haven't done any before. Also look to include regular mobility work and even yoga and Pilates.

By the time you enter your 60s, age, aches, pains and previous injuries may well be taking their toll and you may need to make modifications to your bike set-up. Pay attention to heart and blood pressure health and think about regular checks with your GP.

Keep an eye on your bone health, especially if cycling has been your main sport for a number of years. The lack of impact, although kind on your joints, can result in reduced bone density. Consult with your doctor if you have any concerns.

More cyclists are riding into the 60s, 70s and beyond. In 2017, 105 year old Robert Marchand set an hour record of 22.547km so, there's really no excuse.

🚲 🚲 🚲

You'll probably want to spend some time training on a bike before your trip. The best thing to do is to be realistic about what you can do and create achievable goals then, work your strength up to riding the same daily distances you plan to cover while carrying the same gear you plan to travel with.

Nothing prepares you for a bike tour like "time in the saddle". Even if you excel at other sports and consider yourself a strong athlete, you should try to get out on the bike before your tour; you use a lot of different muscles riding a bike.

You're physically ready if you can do back-to-back day rides that are as long or longer than you are planning for your tour and feel like you could ride again on the third day. One of the pleasures of bike travel is that you'll be riding into progressively better and better shape as you go.

If you're a regular cyclist and / or commuter, keep doing what you're doing. Riding over many days on tour is not necessarily the distance; it's the motivation to keep going day after day, irrespective of your mood or the weather. Commuting by bicycle to work each day in the run-up to a

🚲

long trip is worth its weight in gold, making you go when it looks a bit damp or chilly out there. I've commuted for years, even cycling the same route every day can throw up daily differences.

🚲 🚲 🚲

Of course, you can train specifically for the trip if that's your thing. I never have but I've always cycled anyway and unusually up the mileage a few days prior to leaving.

Begin your training at a mileage that feels comfortable, whether it is 5 miles or 25 miles. Try to ride three to four days per week and gradually increase mileage over the course of a few weeks. By now you'll have some idea of how long you'll be cycling each day – there's your target but bear in mind you will be cycling on a loaded machine.

When training for a tour, riding speed and training heart rate are less important than endurance and time spent on the bike. The goal is to eventually ride several consecutive days (as you will on tour) and spend as much time as possible in the saddle.

🚲

Be sure to take some rides fully loaded, to feel comfortable with the added weight of your touring gear. A fully laden bike feels very different at first, with practice, you should quickly get used to it.

Taking an overnight trip as part of the training (if you've never toured before) will help determine if you've packed wisely and give you a chance to test your equipment while there's still time to make changes or adjustments.

It is important that you avoid overtraining. If you should begin to feel increasingly tired or irritable, or begin to dread riding, you may be training too hard or too often. By the start of your tour, you do not want to feel tired or be suffering from sore knees. Listen to your body and rest when necessary.

Training involves increasing your fitness if you can and more importantly practicing riding in all conditions: on unsurfaced roads and tracks for instance. Try riding along the white line on the side of the road, maintaining your balance as long as possible. Ride in the rain, wind, bright sun and twilight, allow yourself to adjust.

🚲

Even if you're accustomed to long distances, remember that you're probably going to be riding at a leisurely tourist's pace. This means you'll be on your bike longer than you're used to, certainly longer than weekend rides at home.

It's not at all uncommon for people who usually ride at 12 or even 18 mph to average less than 8 mph on a bike tour.

🚲 🚲 🚲

Regular short rides are the fastest way to boost your fitness and improve your cycling performance.

Improving fitness requires the right dosage of training. It needs to be frequent enough to apply some stress, but be balanced and with enough recovery to allow the adaptation process to take place.

If you only have three hours to spare per week you will be able to improve your fitness more with three one-hour sessions, or even several 30-minute rides, than just one long ride.

If you only ride once a week, you may be wondering why, despite your regular rides, you aren't improving. That's because, after just seven days without cycling, your body will

🚲

start to lose some of the fitness gains you have made. To keep progressing and improving fitness, you ideally need to be riding your bike every two-three days. The minimum you can get away with and still see significant fitness gains is three rides a week.

🚲 🚲 🚲

How can I make the process of touring enjoyable?

It's supposed to be a holiday so relax as you ride, and take a break every hour or so. It's not much fun cycling at the expense of all else, you're on holiday and want to enjoy the experience so stop for a snack or visit an attraction.

Make sure you eat frequently, in small amounts and drink enough, if you feel thirsty, it's too late – little and often is key.

Remember to cycle within or just at your limit, listen to your body. Stops for refreshment when needed, water, coffee and cake are king on a tour.

If you don't feel good on the bike, something is wrong. Maybe the placement of the brake levers, the angle of the

🚲

handlebars, reach to the handlebars, seat, or position. Something isn't right and needs to be fixed.

🚲 🚲 🚲

Your bike's gears let you choose different pedaling rates or cadences. Spinning in a gear that is too low is tiring while pushing a gear that is too high is a cause of knee problems. Use all of the gears on your bike – that's what they're there for, using the lighter gears when going up a hill. There is no reason to be a hero and try to reach the top first. Spinning you legs faster in a lighter gear is better for your knees and muscles than slowly grinding in a higher gear.

Any time you feel the slightest twinge of pain in your knees, stop riding. Check saddle height and position to see if an improper adjustment is causing strain on your knees. When you resume riding, check your cadence. Skillful cyclists use a brisk, steady cadence of 70 to 90 pedal revolutions per minute, using the various gears to maintain a constant cadence over varying terrain.

Avoid numb hands (and road rash in the case of a fall) by wearing cycling gloves; gel padding is especially effective and change hand positions frequently as you ride.

188

🚲

🚲 🚲 🚲

The most obvious factor that appeals to fans of cycle touring is that riding a bike is incredibly good for you. Whereas running, jogging and some other high-impact exercise activities can be a bit grueling on your joints, cycling is a low-impact form of exercise.

That's not to say you don't burn plenty of calories whilst pedaling though. Cycling apps will attempt to work out calories burned or calories can be calculated on line, for example caloriesburnedhq.com/calories-burned-biking. It's an inexact science, everybody is different but for an 85kg male cycling for 1 hour at 12 – 14mph, 700 calories could be burned.

If you cycle up hills or off-road, you'll also be working your upper body. What's better than losing weight and keeping fit while on holiday? It means you can eat as much as you like when you reach your evening destination, guilt free. Maybe!

189

🚲

How far can I ride in a day?

This varies depending on your overall fitness, your personal goals, the style of touring you choose and the terrain. As a rule of thumb, depending on flat vs hilly think about:

- Road 40 – 60 miles / 65 – 95km
- Off road 25 – 50 miles / 40 – 80km
- Rugged 15 – 40 miles / 24 – 65km

A day with a mix of terrains will change the expected distance so plan accordingly. It's up to you; you may prefer shorter distances anyway of course.

🚲 🚲 🚲

The next couple of sections might not be relevant to the slower, shorter distance tourer but feel free to read them anyway!

After every ride (and maybe before), make time to stretch and warm up / cool down. Active stretching is best but any stretching you do will contribute to the next day's ride being more manageable and enjoyable.

Warming up is essential to prepare your body and mind to perform at its very best, especially when you are facing a hard effort.

🚲

A warm-up results in a number of physiological responses that are essential for optimal performance. A good analogy is allowing your car engine to warm-up on a cold day. Fuel and oil become more viscous and flows better. Moving parts glide past each other more smoothly and the whole engine performs far more efficiently than if you'd just pressed the accelerator to the floor immediately.

A very important aim of the warm-up is to "switch" your aerobic energy system on prior to you starting your main effort. Doing so means you use energy more efficiently and you are less likely to fatigue prematurely as a result. Your heart rate should be increased progressively, enabling more oxygen to be transported through your blood to and used within the working muscles. With increased body temperature, the range of motion around your joints will also improve and you will get close to your optimal efficiency very quickly.

The consensus is that static stretching before exercise does not prevent injury or enhance performance. In fact, there is some evidence to suggest that static stretching may be detrimental to the rider. A warm-up should prepare the body for the range and type of movement that the activity demands. A rugby player may use bounding and dynamic twists but, for a cyclist, the most appropriate type of warm-up is on the bike.

A cool down helps return your body to its pre-exercise state and will aid recovery and adaptation processes.

A progressive cool-down will help remove metabolic waste products from your muscles. If you don't cool-down, these metabolites will 'sit' there and potentially inhibit recovery. A cool-down will also minimise the likelihood of you feeling dizzy, nauseous or fainting post exercise. It will also allow your blood to redistribute around the body, preventing blood pooled in your lower extremities.

You may find that your body has become stiff after being in a fixed position on the bike for hours and stretching may help your body return to a normal range of movement. The ideal time to spend 5-10 minutes stretching is as soon as you get off the bike, as your muscle temperature will still be elevated and they will be 'more open' to stretching as a result.

🚲

What should I eat and drink?

The view from my camping pod, Paible, Outer Hebrides (2019).

A topic close to my heart, what's the point of touring without coffee and cake stops? Stop mid-morning for coffee and cake – this rule is NOT negotiable! Don't be afraid to take breaks, nobody is watching you to see how "lazy" you are and an hour or more taken out for lunch will restore your energy levels beyond the calorific replacement. There's nothing like a lazy picnic beside a river in France in glorious sunshine – it's part of the tour.

If the bike is the machine then your body is the engine and the engine needs fuel. The best foods for bicycle touring need to replace those lost calories quickly. They also need to be relatively light weight and keep well while on the road. Take care of your body; try to keep a varied diet rich in carbohydrates, proteins, vegetables, salads and fruits and drink plenty of water.

It's important to eat and drink during the ride and also, there's the food when off the bike. I'm reasonably sensible when on the bike, eating and drinking little and often but in the evening, almost anything goes. There will be some purists disagreeing I'm sure but it's supposed to be a fun time after all.

🚲 🚲 🚲

Eating and drinking during the ride.

Muscles work by consuming stores of glycogen (glucose) which is a finite resource and if it is depleted, you will grind

🚲

to a halt. My favourite way of doing this is cake and ice cream! I've yet to feel guilty over eating cake and ice cream on a tour.

The cyclists' name for grinding to a halt is "to bonk"; suddenly there's nothing left in the tank with the legs turning to jelly and each pedal stroke is a huge effort.

A bonk (yes it's a noun and a verb!) happens when glycogen stores are depleted during long rides or those of a high intensity.

The body can store about 300–400g of glycogen in the muscles and about 120g in the liver (sciencedaily.com/terms/glycogen.htm). During a ride, this translates to about 1,200 calories of energy. If you don't replenish this on the bike, you'll deplete your reserves fairly quickly; at a moderate intensity, cyclists can burn up to 800 calories an hour.

Eating will replace the glycogen but the body can only absorb about 60g per hour.

Pace yourself by riding at a low intensity during efforts lasting longer than two hours.

🚲

It's enough to drink one sports drink and one energy bar per hour or a big slice of Victoria sponge! Make sure you have a decent breakfast and use the evening meal as an opportunity to replace glycogen.

When touring, I carry all sorts of snacks, these include:

- Nuts and Raisins (trail mix); these are an ideal snack to munch on whilst cycling. Whilst they may not offer much in the way of instant carb release (apart from the raisins), they keep the body fuelled with fats and protein from the nuts
- Bananas; a cyclist's favourite – 120 cals of carbs
- Health / cereal bars
- Almonds; sold in bags in most supermarkets, easy to eat a handful.

I also carry some energy balls kindly made for me by my youngest daughter, very tasty (purelykaylie.com/chocolate-coconut-energy-balls).

Never pass up a water stop if there is even the slightest chance (or uncertainty) about its availability for the rest of the day(s) ahead. Water is THE important ingredient in being able to continue riding – once you've had to tough it out with a parched throat until the next water-stop; this lesson is learned and respected forever.

Most cafes and bars will gladly top up your Bidons. I'm not a fan of buying bottled water but needs must sometimes. Buy decent quality water bottles so your water doesn't taste of plastic and stays cool.

🚲 🚲 🚲

With the human body composed of approximately 60% water, it should be no surprise that you need to keep it topped up with fluid to perform optimally.

Studies have shown that surprisingly low fluid losses can significantly affect your ability to ride. Only a 2% drop in body weight due to sweating (1.6kg for an 80kg rider) will impair performance noticeably, more will create additional problems.

Drink before you feel thirsty and monitor urine colour, straw colour is perfect. Drink little and often right from the start of your ride.

🚲

It is possible to drink too much water and if you're not also taking on adequate electrolytes, you'll effectively dilute and affect the balance of your body's fluids.

🚲 🚲 🚲

Eating and drinking when off the bike.

Always eat breakfast before you start because you never know if there will be something on your route to fuel yourself when you need it.

I always have a good breakfast, if camping, the first thing we do after striking camp is to find breakfast. We also use this time to agree the plan for the day and if staying in a B&B, there's always as much food as you can eat so, obviously, I take full advantage! I think our record remains at three breakfasts on one day!

The most popular bike touring food include; oats, Peanut Butter (not a fan personally), pasta, rice, lentils, bread, cheese and noodles.

Having said all this, provided you have a good breakfast, regular snacks and a decent evening meal, what you eat and drink isn't hugely important for the casual, fairly low mileage,

🚲

short term tourist. Cycling with a banging hangover isn't a huge amount of fun though!

Carrying food on your bike.

A few packets of nuts or some cereal bars will fit almost anywhere on the bike, usually I return home with a few misshapen but perfectly edible cereal bars! You may wish to carry food if you're cooking at night; some foods present more of a problem than others.

Water bottles can be used for dried food. They are already waterproof, don't weigh too much and in the event that they are dropped, don't open up and spill the contents everywhere.

Rice and oats are the best things to store in drinks bottles, followed by spaghetti and pasta.

Ice cream cartons or plastic take away boxes are great for using to stow anything which might be squashed in a pannier. Don't take anything which will need to be kept cold or cool. Once in France, my friend bought his wife an elaborate chocolate creation for her birthday. After cycling for a couple more days in glorious sunshine he ended up with a brown lump in the bottom of his pannier. Luckily it was in a plastic

199

🚲

bag. We saved him the embarrassment of having to take it home by helping him eat it. Bags of ice can split, ask another of my cycling colleagues, he was drying his wet kit most of the next day!

Finding a shop or petrol station open until late is usually not much of a problem in the UK. Many shops will be open on Sunday.

Where you will struggle to find shops are in the more rural areas where many village shops have been lost and in the more remote and sparsely populated areas of the UK such as in the north and the northwest of Scotland. I fell foul of the Sunday trading laws on a Sunday on the Isle of Lewis; absolutely nothing is open except in Stornaway where, luckily, I spent the night. France shuts on Sunday and very often on Monday; again, I've been caught out with shut shops and bars miles from nowhere in France on a Monday.

How do I stay safe and secure?

A Sustrans sign; Coast and Castles (2020).

Don't be alarmed, in years of cycle touring I've never had an issue with security; no thefts and I've never felt unsafe. I have toured only in northern Europe but worldwide some countries are safer than others.

It pays to take some sensible precautions however.

I've already mentioned I'd recommend taking a good lock and a cable or two locks, especially if you're going through urban areas. It's better to lug around a 1kg lock than lose your bike; it might also be a requirement for insurance claims. A D-lock and cable works to lock two bike wheels and frame to something sturdy i.e. a Sheffield Stand ("M" or "U" shaped stands) in a well-lit and busy location. Locks are categorised as bronze, silver and gold; you get what you pay for with a lock and many locks can be carried on the frame of the bike. YouTube has some good videos explaining how to best lock your bike and cyclinguk.org has some excellent tips and hints.

Take pictures of your bike including any scratches or marks for identification, record the frame number and keep receipts. Hopefully you won't need it but consider insurance. Even if you already have a fairly good travel policy, some explicitly exclude cycle touring from cover.

It's possible to register your bike online which could help tracking it down in the unlikely event of theft, check out bikeregister.com or the phone app Found as examples.
If you have a travel insurance policy, read the small print carefully. Some policies don't cover off-road riding; others don't include theft of cycling accessories and most won't repatriate your bike in a medical emergency. Some companies offer cycling-specific insurance, if you plan to go cycle touring regularly and independently, it might be worth

considering. Personally I have insurance via my membership of British Cycling to cover liability (often provided as part of your home or travel insurance) and theft.

Also, consider etching your postcode onto your bike frame and remove the saddle and take it with you, leather Brooks saddles proving very popular with thieves. I made a permanent anchor from my Brooks saddle to frame with an old bike chain fed through an inner tube. Having said all this, in many years of bike touring, I've never had any issues with thieves, indeed on the Outer Hebrides; locals were surprised I actually wanted to lock my bike as nothing was routinely locked on the islands.

If camping in remote areas, lock your bike to a tent pole overnight, or use it as a structural component of your tent, if someone comes after your bike, they'll likely wake you up.

If you enter a shop or restaurant, lock your bike near a window so you can keep tabs on it while shopping or eating.

Don't advertise flashy, expensive-looking bicycles, components and gear. Some long-distance cycle tourists will spray paint an expensive frame to make it look unattractive.

⛢

When you are not with your bike, keep all critical valuables on your person (wallet, passport, camera, etc.). Handlebar bags and daypacks can be easily detached so you take them with you.

As mentioned before, if you're booking accommodation, always ask if they can store your bike. I've never had a problem with this and the chosen accommodation has always been keen to help. I've left my bike in sheds, basements and also taken it into my room. Many budget hotels are fine for you to do this, ask for a ground floor room.

Should the worse happen, call the police and have a formal report written up. You will need this for any insurance claims; hopefully your wallet and passport are on your person.

🚲 🚲 🚲

Share any planning with someone home based, tell them where you are going and when you will be back. Even if that means texting someone your route details and expected time of arrival back home, let them know when you are back safe and sound. My wife likes to know where I'll be each evening and a quick check in call or text puts her mind at ease.

204

🚲

Consider sharing your location sharing via your Smartphone, apps such as WhatsApp have this feature. It's called Live Location and allows you to share your real-time location for a specific amount of time. WhatsApp claim this feature is end-to-end encrypted, which means no one can see your live location except the people you share with.

What3words is a geolocating app that uses a three-word code to locate anywhere on earth. The downloadable app works by splitting the entire planet into three-metre by three-metre squares, which are then given a unique three-word code. That gives a rapid, simple and relatively foolproof way of sharing any location, which is coming in very handy for emergency services teams.

🚲 🚲 🚲

I've mentioned helmets and hi viz already, assuming you're an adult then make up your own mind on these issues.

The vast majority of people in this world are good; when you travel solo you'll really see that for yourself. People will offer you food, a safe place to stay, mechanical support, a kind chat. If any person or situation makes you feel

🚲

uncomfortable, trust your gut and remove yourself from that situation however you can.

On a group cycling trip to France, I was in the lead by a couple of minutes. While waiting for my buddies to catch up, I was hailed by a lady who was standing having a fag. She asked me if I would go with her into her house and help her move something. Fearing I was going to be abducted and tortured, I cannily waited for the rest so we could all be abducted and tortured together. It turned out she wanted us to help move some carpets into two rooms in the large house that she was renovating as a Chambre d'Hote. She gave us a tour of the whole, large place and a couple of beers. She spoke no English, but was very pleasant and enthusiastic. Sometimes first impressions aren't true impressions!

🚲 🚲 🚲

Bike maintenance is key; a regular check (as in "M" or ABC mentioned earlier) will go a long way to ensure a trouble free trip. You can't legislate for bad luck or punctures however.

I don't want this to turn into me preaching but, it makes sense to obey local traffic laws and be aware of what's going

🚲

on around you when riding; don't wear headphones while cycling.

Keep an eye out for potholes! Seemingly beautifully laid stretches of road can have potholes appear from nowhere and you only need to hit one and you could have an accident. This is true for stones and other debris such as branches.

Cycling too fast on a loaded bicycle when bike touring is not an issue many people face, except in one particular situation – going downhill. After time grinding up a hill, it can be tempting to let loose and just go down the other side as fast as you can, but common sense says to keep it under control. On my Coast and Castles trip, I rode over the Moorfoot Hills in the rain and in spite of using my brakes, I touched 55kph a couple of times on the downhill towards Edinburgh, luckily it was a lovely smooth road. Exhilarating but I didn't feel 100% in control at all times!

When passing vehicles, especially big trucks, be aware of any blind spots they may have. The simple rule of thumb, is if you can't see the driver (either in their mirrors or through a window), they can't see you. Cyclists can run into trouble when cycling down the side of a long vehicle which is about to turn.

One of the greatest dangers to cyclists is that of being "doored". This could happen when cycling too closely alongside a row of parked cars so make sure you're always at least a door's width away (1.5m) at all times, no matter where that puts you in the road.

At a junction or roundabout, assume the middle of the lane to prevent vehicles trying to come alongside.

A cardinal rule of cycling is to brake before you have to, especially on curves and downhills. Brake just before going into a curve; then, if you need to slow down more, brake gently with the rear brake while in the curve. Always apply brakes gradually. Never slam on just the front brake, or you'll fly over the handlebars!

Use both brakes to slow down or stop. The stopping power of the rear brake is about 75% of the front brake and 65% of both brakes being applied at the same time.

Brake in a rhythmic on-again-off-again pattern, squeezing both brakes firmly for a few seconds and then releasing the brakes for a few seconds. Continuous braking will glaze the surface of the brake pads and result in loss of stopping power.

Don't begin your tour without practicing emergency braking. This entails three motions performed simultaneously: (1) Shifting your weight toward the rear of the saddle, while (2) moving your hands onto the brake handles and (3) applying firm, even pressure to both brakes.

Things to do before leaving and after returning home.

Checking out a fountain near the Elbe (2011).

Before you leave

Make sure you sort out anything you'd normally do prior to a trip away. There may be a couple of different things you might want to consider prior to a fully loaded bike tour however.

Make final purchases of clothing and equipment.

Make certain that all repairs and maintenance, including lubrication, are made on your bike and perform a final "M" check. It's better to discover and take care of problems before your tour begins.

Buy an extra pair of glasses, or contacts and get a copy of your prescription.

Continue any training rides you might be doing, seeking hills and varied terrain, attempt to simulate the type of riding you may encounter on your tour and do some rides with fully loaded packs to test for proper weight distribution.

Pack and repack your gear a couple of times.

Make arrangements for paying any monthly bills coming due during your absence.

Make sure you have used all your equipment and know how it works.

Pick up your travel tickets; have you printed your boarding pass?

Fill medical prescriptions to last longer than your trip.

Can you be contacted; does someone have a copy of your itinerary, is someone feeding the cat?

🚲

When I return home.

When you return home, unpack your stuff as soon as possible, you don't want to be leaving a wet tent rolled up in a bag for months on end, or it will rot and smell.

Attack the mountain of washing!

Air your sleeping bag etc. It's surprising how "I will leave it a day" turns into leaving it for a week!

Label your photos, they might be fresh in the memory for a few days, but as time goes by, you may start forgetting where they were taken.

I write notes while I'm away, jot down thoughts both to remind me of (hopefully) a great trip and to serve as a "lessons learned" for the next one. Did I take too much stuff or too little, what would I do differently next time? In addition to being a nice reminder of your first experience traveling by bicycle, it will help you when you need to make recommendations to other people in the future.

Start planning your next trip!

About the author

Outer Hebrides (2019).

For as long as I can remember I've cycled, to school, university (when it wasn't the trendy thing to do), places of work, nights out and more recently on holiday. Living in Bristol, despite the hills it's often the quickest and cheapest way to get around.

Following many years in IT, I left permanent employment in 2004 to enter the world of contract project management spending time labouring in the offices of many household names across the south west.

213

Turning 60 in 2017, I decided enough was enough and it was time to slow down, well, at least to try something new.

Following a chance meeting a few years ago (whilst cycling), I was asked if I'd like to train as a cycling instructor. After qualifying in October 2017 I've been working part time in schools and with adults on a 1 to 1 basis. It's quite a cool thing to tell people you're a "professional cyclist".

Other things that keep me busy are watching Southampton FC and Bristol Bears rugby, holidays, cycling, running and pub quizzes.

I live in Bristol with my teacher wife and three daughters in their 20s and I can be found on Facebook, Twitter; @peteradcock8 and Instagram; peteradcockcycling.

Acknowledgements

Yours truly in Brittany (2017).

My long suffering family allowing me the time and space to go and do these things, they do have full access to the TV remote while I'm away and apparently the "house is much tidier and quieter while you were away" so that wasn't all bad.

My wife for proof reading, tactfully suggesting changes and helping me make sense of it all.

My daughters for helping me with the technical Instagram stuff.

🚲

All the wonderful B&B owners, hoteliers, camp site owners for always being so welcoming.

Everybody I've met over the years be they cyclists, visitors to the area, or locals, who have been, almost without exception charming, engaging, helpful, interested and interesting.

Other titles by the same author

All available on Amazon in either book or kindle format or both.

Cycling the Hebridean Way 10 islands, causeways and cake

Six days cycling across the Outer Hebrides, my first solo cycle tour and first cycle tour in the UK. Wonderful scenery, warm and welcoming people, plenty of cake, superb views, one hill, ferries, wildlife and beaches to die for. I scribbled some notes and have now got around to getting them into some sort of logical order. Go and do this, you don't have to be a hardened 100 mile a day cyclist, my biggest day was only 35 miles, be prepared for all weathers and I defy you not to have the best time.

Paperback edition: 138 pages; ISBN-10: 1655585959; ISBN-13: 978-1655585951; Dimensions: 15.2 x 0.9 x 22.9 cm

Kindle edition: File Size: 821KB; 109 pages; ASIN: B083GZRV32

Kobo edition: ISBN: 1230003670552; Download options: EPUB 2 (DRM-Free)

🚲 🚲 🚲

Cycling Coast and Castles South - 2020: Cycling in a pandemic

🚲

2020 was the year of Covid, a pandemic which brought us lockdown. Foreign travel was next to impossible but in summer, the UK started to open up and we were encouraged to holiday at home. After a false start, I decided to cycle the spectacular Coast and Castles south from Tynemouth to Edinburgh. This took me through some of the north east's industrial heritage, I saw spectacular beaches, the glorious Tweed Valley, the damp Moorfoot hills and of course castles, lots of castles. Fuelled by coffee and ice cream, this is my account of 5 superb days of cycling in this wonderful corner of our island.

Paperback edition: 145 pages, ISBN-13: 979-8688720792
Kindle edition: File Size: 5407KB; 147 pages; ASIN: B08JVFF1M4

🚲 🚲 🚲

Cycle touring in France and Germany: A selection of notes

For the last 9 years, 4 friends and I have made cycling expeditions to France and Germany and pottered along various cycle ways, rivers, canals, disused railways and small roads (apart from one mad cycle across Paris). During the trips we jotted down some notes which have languished on

🚲

hard drives or on dusty sheets of paper. This is an attempt to pull them all together, add some more information and publish in the hope they may be useful to others considering similar trips. The adventures were: France: 2012: The river Loire - Nevers to Angers; 2014: La Rochelle to Bordeaux; 2015: Circular expedition east of Bordeaux; 2016: Bordeaux – Cognac – Bordeaux; 2017: St Malo - Rennes - St Malo; 2019: Montpellier and Germany; 2011: Cycling the Elbe; 2013: Cycling the Black Forest Cycle Way; 2018: Cycling the Weser-Radweg - Hann. Münden to Minden. Don't expect 100s of km a day, more relaxed journey looking at interesting places and sampling the local delicacies.

Paperback edition: 340 pages; ISBN-13: 979-8635586709; ASIN: B086Y3S9GB; **Kindle edition:** File Size: 983KB; 215 pages; ASIN: B086XDGL8J

🚲 🚲 🚲

Cycle touring in France: A selection of notes

A collection of notes (with enhancements) from 6 cycle tours in France in the areas of Bordeaux, La Rochelle, St Malo, Rennes, the Loire valley and Montpellier. Tales of 5 friends pottering from 0 km to 50 km a day depending on how we

🚲

felt. A good mix of hiring bikes, taking our own bikes and camping. Hopefully some of these trips may inspire the reader to attempt something similar.

Paperback edition: 217 pages; ISBN-13; 979-8633995602; ASIN: B086PPJHVN; **Kindle edition:** File Size; 987KB; 151 pages; ASIN: B086RS9L2W

🚲 🚲 🚲

Cycle touring in Germany: A selection of notes

A collection of notes (with enhancements) from 3 cycle tours in Germany along the river Elbe (Elbe Radweg), the Black Forest Cycle Way (Südschwarzwald-Radweg) and the river Weser (Weser Radweg). Tales of 5 friends pottering from 0 km to 50 km a day depending on where we had to be that evening. A good mix of hiring bikes, taking our own bikes and camping. Hopefully some of these trips may inspire the reader to attempt something similar.

Paperback edition: 139 pages; ISBN-13: 979-8635614860; ASIN: B086Y39JBZ; **Kindle edition:** File Size: 891KB; 87 pages; ASIN: B086SG1TZF

🚲 🚲 🚲

🚲

Cycling around Bordeaux - Three Routes in Western France

An account of 5 intrepid souls and 3 cycling trips in the Bordeaux area of western France. Firstly, La Rochelle to Bordeaux, secondly a loop from Bordeaux using part of the Roger Lapébie cycle path and thirdly a loop from Bordeaux to Cognac returning to Bordeaux. An adventure in the sun, getting lost, fearing kidnap, pleasant cycling, wine, cheese and putting the world to rights.

Kindle edition only: File Size: 898KB; 63 pages; ASIN: B085VFZ38Q

🚲 🚲 🚲

Cycling the Black Forest Cycle Way (Südschwarzwald-Radweg): Adventures in three countries - 2013

A cycling tour of the southern Black Forest cycle way (the Südschwarzwald-Radweg) from Frieburg to Basel, a detour into France and back to Freiburg. A story of wonderful scenery, lovely people, border crossings and unnecessarily transporting a pineapple.

Kindle edition only: File Size: 797KB; 32 pages; ASIN: B086417J9F

221

🚲

🚲 🚲 🚲

The river Loire - Nevers to Angers, châteaux and cheese

In 2012 it was decided 5 of us would celebrate our friend's looming 60th birthday by undertaking a long distance cycle ride - slowly! This is a tale of cycling the western part of the Loire valley i.e. the flat bit, more chateaux then you can shake a baguette at, wine, cheese and camping on islands in the stream.

Kindle edition only: File Size: 850KB; 45 pages; ASIN: B085VHX1LD

🚲 🚲 🚲

Cycling in Brittany - a short trip from St Malo to Rennes - 2017

A short trip cycling from St Malo, west along the coast via Dinard, then south to Rennes via Dinan along a Voie Vert. A train ride north from Rennes and a gentle cycle west to St Malo. An easy trip to do in a few days with plenty of options to detour. Some of it could be done in a long weekend.

Kindle edition only: File Size: 886KB; 37 pages; ASIN: B086N3PD6M

🚲

🚲 🚲 🚲

Cycling around Montpellier - Coping with the heat - 2019

A trip to and from Montpellier in southern France. Our original plan was curtailed due to record breaking temperatures of over 40C. Not a huge amount of cycling but much swimming in the sea and campsite pools but these notes give the reader a flavour of possible routes around this area.

Kindle edition only: File Size: 996KB; 30 pages; ASIN: B086RQK9SR

🚲 🚲 🚲

Cycling the Weser-Radweg: Hann. Münden to Minden - 2018

A 220km ride along part of the river Weser cycle way (Weser Radweg) from Hann. Munden to Mindon via Hamburg. Lovely flat cycling, some beautiful villages, great camp sites and plenty of beer.

Kindle edition only: File Size: 953KB; 30 pages; ASIN: B086RW6PXB

🚲

゛゙゛゙ ゛゙゛゙ ゛゙゛゙

Cycling the Elbe Cycle Route (Elberadweg): Lutherstadt Wittenberg to the Czech border - 2011

A trip along 220km of the Elbe cycle way to the Czech border via Berlin. Much beer to drink and wonderful cycling. Considering this was our first experience of taking bikes on a plane, it all went very well.

Kindle edition only: File Size: 671KB; 33 pages; ASIN: B086SDCSF

゛゙゛゙

Printed in Great Britain
by Amazon

65320215R00129